FINDING THE GREAT CREATIVE
YOU

A Seven Step Adventure

by
Lynne Garnett, Ph.D.
with
Patricia Cramer

Aslan Publishing
310 Blue Ridge Drive
Boulder Creek, CA 95006
(408) 338-7504

Published by

Aslan Publishing
310 Blue Ridge Drive
Boulder Creek, CA 95006
(408) 338-7504

Garnett, Lynne. 1942-
    Finding the great creative you: a seven step adventure / by Lynne
Garnett.
        p. cm.
    Includes bibliographical references.
    ISBN 0-944031-06-4 : S18.95. -- ISBN 0-944031-05-6 (pbk.) : S10.95
    1. Self-actualization (Psychology).   2. Self-actualization
(Psychology)--Problems, exercises, etc.   I. Title.
    BF637.S4G88   1989
158'.1--dc20   89-77300
                                                                      CIP

© 1990, Lynne Garnett

The acknowledgements page constitutes an extension of the copyright page.
Quotations from the article, "They Call Him A Miracle Doctor" are
reprinted with permission from *Parade* magazine, © 1988,
from the author, Michael Ryan, and the author's agents,
Scott Meredith Literary Agency, Inc., 845 Third Ave., New York, NY 10022.

Cover design by Brenda Plowman
Printed in USA
First Edition

10 9 8 7 6 5 4 3 2 1

Dedication

To my greatest teacher,
my Mom
and, in memoriam,
to my Dad

*The longest journey is the journey inward
of him who has chosen his destiny.*

Dag Hammarskjold

Contents

Welcome to the greatest adventure you'll every have: your own life! It's time for a new beginning, and the recognition of your own courage and peak experiences.

Discover who you are at the center of your individuality and strength. Find the fulfilled you that you have always known exists, the magic that you share with very trusted friends at very special times.

Each of us is born with a great Purpose for being here. Find out what that Purpose is and how you would live it out if you had absolutely no blocks in your life. Go past survival to your highest vision.

We all have blocks that prevent us from being the best we can be and doing the best we can do. Find out what your personal blocks are and unlock their energy to work for you rather than against you.

Discover the sources of your personal power, then learn how to increase that power exponentially through focus. Learn to get all your energy working in the same direction.

There is no change without a firm commitment to act. This step commits us to making the choice to take the steps necessary to move powerfully ahead. We sign a contract with ourselves to practice persistence and succeed.

This step provides training and practice in the skills of mental visioning and affirmation to reinforce the power of your choices and increase your inner strength. We train our thinking to support our Purpose.

Without a specific plan to put into action, you will end up where you started. This is where the plan comes together. You identify the steps to take in order to fully live your creative Passion.

Acknowledgements

I would like to acknowledge the very special people who have influenced my life and in turn, this book.

The person who has always reminded me that I can make the most of my life and be the very best that I can be is my mom, Virginia Wolfe.

Dawson Church, my publisher, demonstrated a deep commitment to *Finding the Great Creative You*, providing untold hours of dedicated love, editing and support for the book. Brenda Plowman offered constant balance and support, especially through stressful times. Lionel is the special child whose beautiful spirit inspired the infant visualization. He is one of the wise children who now blesses our earth.

Many people have made significant contributions to the fabric of my life. My closest friend, Dr. Luci Carstens, has always been my cheerleader and reality checker. Sarah Wilson Jurak has shown me the way to a whole new level of personal trust and success. Dr. Linda Nishigaya offers a model of clear-mindedness and integrity, and Kathe Paulson walks the path of the heart.

Dr. Barbara Newton demonstrated the excellent good taste to hire me at West Oahu College, and became a good friend. Holly Yamada and Dr. Jean Yamada in their own very special ways have been my teachers. Jane Ann Pullen was there in the toughest times, and Janet Brown kept the faith.

Sally Hermann always has a good word and Carol Burnham and Bob Paca encourage. My love and thanks to all of my colleagues (students and teachers) from West Oahu College, Pearl City, Hawaii. They provided unconditional love and support.

Dr. Zev Wanderer guided my clinical training and is a dear friend. Dr. Bob Alberti and Dr. Michael Emmons guided my work in assertiveness training and supported my early writing in the field of psychology.

I appreciate the inspiration provided by the lives of all those special people, the Pathwalkers, who I interviewed for the book, and those who allowed me to quote their words: Dr. Ken Blanchard, author of *The One Minute Manager*; Lucy Beale, co-author of *The Win/Win Way*; Dr. Larry Wilson, author of *Changing the Game: The New Way to Sell;* Barbara Peace, artist; Thea Alexander, author of *2150 A.D.*, Dr Charles Garfield, researcher and author of *Peak Performers; The New Heroes of American Business;* Carrie and Mark Greenwald who are dedicated to the re-greening of the earth and Joyce Filupeit, corporate trainer.

To Marlene Bennet, an inspiring friend, Mike Speakman, Beverly Allen, Irene Falk, Claire, Lorrie Cade, Scott Anderson and Dr. Karl Jurak who offered their personal stories. To those people who allowed me to quote from their books and works, including Dr. Morris Massey, Pam Lontos, Charles Wedemeyer and to *Elipse,* the Shanti Project Newsletter for the interview with Dr. Charles Garfield. Thanks also to the Institute of Noetic Sciences for permission to quote details of the Marilyn King story on page 129 from the Summer 1985 issue of the *Noetic Sciences Review.*

Special thanks to Diana Soto who suggested Aslan Publishing, and to Kaye Settle who loaned me her Mac. Greg Hogland of Alpha Graphics helped me with disk translations. I appreciate my attorney Mervyn Braude, who cared for and protected my work. Thanks to Patricia Cramer, who edited the first drafts and knew my material would be a success.

And finally, much love and thanks to three young teachers, Courtney, Missy and Gary, and their dad, Herbert, who gave me a family and expanded my life knowledge.

You are never given a wish without also being given the power to make it come true. You may have to work at it however.

Richard Bach, "The Bridge Across Forever"

Preface

Life without Passion

To live life fully we must have Passion. Without it we merely exist. In 1963 I worked for a large insurance firm as an account clerk. Clerks, claims adjustors and account managers all worked in one large room, our desks aligned in rows, like galley slaves.

Our supervisor was situated in a little glass cage at the front of the room. He was a loud and intimidating man; not a person to inspire or motivate. There was another man, quiet and gray, who had worked for this company all of his productive life and was within five years of retirement. About seven years previously he had been "promoted" to a desk by the window. The window overlooked a dirty city street. More than once this poor man was berated publicly by the supervisor. I asked him why he took this abuse without complaint. He said that I was "too young to understand"; that his "security depended on compliance."

I was working for this company the day President Kennedy was assassinated. The event moved everybody in the office deeply. But the gray man's only comment was, "Why did a rich man like that want to be President anyway?" The destitution of his own emotional life had left him barren of concern, even for the President of his own country.

These events profoundly shaped my life. Although I spent many years living in economic fear, I would always ultimately make decisions based on spiritual rather than economic survival. It was the subtle picture of this man, sad and bitter, that hung in the recesses of my mind and spurred me on to fill my life with living. I didn't want to find out after I died that life had to do with joy and giving. I knew that life had to be about doing our best, living with honor and trusting life to take care of us in return. When we do what we love, encourage ourselves and live with integrity, we already have everything we'll ever need.

We have all been given more than mere survival capabilities. We

---

Life is an adventure, or it is nothing at all.

Helen Keller

are endowed with opportunities, capabilities and personal honor. Living honorably may seem the more difficult path, but ultimately it is what makes life worthwhile. When we live from the fullness of ourselves, from the depths of our greater being, we are more than a conglomerate of cells. We are the grandest experiment ever; we are consciousness, joy, energy and intelligence. We are the embodiment of creation; we are life itself.

Life with Passion

The effect of the depth of despair of the elderly gray man was a stepping stone toward the empowerment of my own life. Inadvertently he offered himself as an object lesson in the power of consciousness. When I have found myself financially and emotionally challenged it has always been when I have lost faith with myself and wallowed in self-pity and fear. I remember the gray man and I reread a quote that has been a guide to overcoming fear. The quote reminds me that the power to overcome fear comes from within. It comes from Frank Herbert's masterpiece, *Dune:* "I must not fear. Fear is the mind-killer. Fear is the little death that brings total obliteration. I will face my fear. I will permit it to pass over me and through me. And when it has gone past I will turn the inner eye to see its path. Where the fear has gone there will be nothing. Only I will remain."

My own life has been a series of wonderful opportunities for growth and learning. I've had the opportunity to be a business professional, manager and corporate trainer. I've had the opportunity to be a clinical psychologist, career counselor and social worker. I've worked and studied in Japan, Malaysia and Mexico. I've traveled in Russia, China and Europe. I owned a successful company in Hawaii and I am now a successful entrepreneur in the Northwest. Has it been easy going all the way? Not by a long shot. I have managed to learn it all the hard way. The key is: never let them get you down. You can do it.

Some people say–jokingly, I hope–that I have had so many careers because I can't hold a job. I see that same feature as representing creativity and a willingness to risk. I have taken each promising opportunity that came my way. Each change in my career direction has been built on the previous opportunity.

Everyone has a potential, in essence, built into them. And if we are to live life to its fullest, we must realize that potential.

Norman Vincent Peale

No experience is ever lost and no lesson learned is ever wasted. It is essential that we understand that life is a learning process. We are never "completed" or "finished." "Life is the only true finishing school," as Yogi Berra once said "and it isn't over till it's over."

When you have a sense of your overall Purpose in life you are better able to grasp the opportunities that come your way because you are clear on your direction. My greater Purpose in life is to help people be all that they can be. If I catch myself indulging in negative or fearful thinking, I can regain control of my life by focusing on what is most important, seeing the up-side of the situation and dedicating my energies to positive action. It would be just as easy to go the other way, to let the fear take hold, to think negatively and to become frozen with anxiety, but I don't. I use my mind to work for me rather than against me and I stay in control of my life.

Change and Risk

We are in a time of rapid change in all areas of our lives: business, relationships, finance and international politics. Those who are able to let go of old concepts of "security" and "stability" will move on to new and different ways of thinking about work, success and life. They will have the ability to grow with change rather than be negatively affected by it. Change causes loss of the old ways, but it also offers the opportunities of the future.

Every day I work with corporations that are trying to change their cultures to create an environment where people are valued for their contributions. The new corporate philosophies encourage intrepreneurship and creativity. The success of business today depends on the development of a committed, motivated and creative work population. We will not make it through these changes without respect for others, self-respect, courage, integrity and a sense of personal responsibility.

More and more people are beginning to make the risky shift to self-fulfillment. Corporate people, entrepreneurs, artists, farmers, inventors, and other professionals are taking more responsibility for their destinies. It is essential that each one of us take a very close look at how we are going to spend the major part of our lives. The work we

---

The question is not "Why are we here?" but
"How should we live our lives?"

Mortimer Adler

do, the careers we choose, the personal path or direction that we take in our lives will determine the quality of our lives.

Risk is an essential part of living life fully and with passion. Throughout the years many people have added their stories to the fabric of my life. As I have worked with them, been friends with them, learned from them, they have helped me to focus on the Purpose of my life. The writer Jean-Paul Sartre said that "Hell is living with other people." Actually, life is about people and living life fully with them. We owe our aliveness to interacting with others and with our world.

This book is a journey of personal exploration to find our own guiding Purpose in life and the expression of that purpose which is our Passion. Our Passion is our work and that work might be parenting, artistry, corporate management or owning our own company. Our work as our Passion will be the most fulfilling and most satisfying choice for our lives.

Let's begin the journey together.

To live is not merely to breathe, it is to act; it is to make use of our organs, senses, faculties, of all those parts of ourselves which give us a feeling of existence.

Jean-Jacques Rousseau

Preparing
for
Adventure!

How Valuable Is Your Life?

Dr. Benjamin Carson is an award-winning surgeon and humanitarian. He is known as the Miracle Worker. Dr. Carson's less-than-auspicious beginnings started 36 years ago in an inner city slum. His parents were divorced and his mother worked several jobs to support Ben and his older brother. The most important thing that Mrs. Carson did for her boys was to convince them that they could make something of their lives, even if their environment continually told them they couldn't.

As a youngster Ben had a very bad temper. As a young black man in the inner city he often felt angry and out-of-control. If anyone infringed on his rights he retaliated with rocks, hammers, bottles and knives. During one outburst, he stabbed another teenager with a camping knife. Fortunately for both boys, the knife broke on the other boy's belt buckle, essentially saving two lives. As he began to think about what he had done and what the consequences could have been, Ben found himself at a turning point and he began to change his life.

In junior high school Benjamin Carson went to school outside of the inner city, away from the old influences. He did very well and won a prize as the best student. However, by high school he was back in the inner city, back to the pressures of his friends and his environment. He

---

Let's stop equating work with earning a living, but rather think of it as an important component of making a life.

Ralph C. Weinrich, "Michigan Business Review"

wanted to be a part of the crowd and the crowd was into alcohol and other drugs. His once bright future began to pale. To her great credit, his mother kept after him. Benjamin began to study hard and ultimately won a scholarship to Yale.

At Yale Ben ran into another stumbling block, inadequate study habits. His skills had been fine for high school but they were not good enough to keep him ahead at university. He worked to improve and turned himself in what he calls "an in-depth learner." He says, "I never, under any circumstances, thought of giving up on anything I do."

Dr. Benjamin Carson graduated, went through his internship and obtained a number of prestigious positions in his field. In 1986 Dr. Carson became director of pediatric neurosurgery at Johns Hopkins Children's Center. He has performed rare brain operations that have saved the lives of hydrocephalic children, including one operation performed in the womb! He was also part of a team that separated Siamese twins who were joined at the skull and shared major blood systems in the brain. The operation left both children alive and intact.

Dr. Carson is known as a man of compassion, decency and courage. Despite his busy surgical schedule, he flies all over the United States to speak to school children. He tells them to take responsibility for their lives. He tells them that education gives them independence and the ability to control their own destiny: "The big difference between people who succeed and people who don't is not that the ones who are successful don't have barriers and obstacles. Everybody has barriers and obstacles. If you look at them as containing fences that don't allow you to advance, then you're going to be a failure. If you look at them as hurdles that strengthen you each time you go over one, then you're going to be a success."

Your Life Is as Valuable as You Make It

We are by design beings that are powerful, alive, aware, joyful, competent and loving. We are entities of intelligence and energy who are meant to have a boundless zest for life. We are meant to be happy and full of joy, living and working in ways that make us feel worthwhile. We are meant to be the very best that we can be.

When we sense mild or serious dissatisfaction with the quality of our lives; when we lose ourselves to the feverish activity of everyday life; when we lose touch with that center of peaceful calm that keeps us balanced and in control of our selves, we become frustrated and anxious. We develop a sense of life being "out of order." We become angry that things are not "going the way they should," meaning "our way." We may feel abused, bitter and fearful. This tension and anxiety feed upon themselves and create more and more unhappiness.

The unhappiness that we hold inside goes against our Purpose, our reason for existing on this earth. Each personal Purpose is a part of our universal purpose, to leave this world a better place than we found it.

When we are frustrated, angry and hurt, we can easily believe that what happens to us is outside of our control. Yet the fact is that we are always in control, even when we choose to give that control away. At any moment we can decide, like Dr. Benjamin Carson, to guide our own life in a positive direction. The choice is always ours.

Peak Experiences

We have all experienced feeling fully alive, being at our very best. We have special moments, times when we transcend our normal selves and exceed our own expectations. These are called **peak experiences.** Peak experiences are crystal clear moments of success, joy and personal fulfillment. In these moments we are so touched by some event in our lives that we are transported beyond the mundane.

It is essential for us to know that rather than being occasional events, peak experiences are meant to be a constant feature of our lives. It is these very experiences that shape who we are as people by reinforcing our inner sense of strength, courage and joy.

Peak experiences take many forms. Remember the instant you held your newborn child and saw in that perfect little face a replica of your own? Recall the moment you were told of a promotion that you had worked for so diligently. Think about the time of perfect sharing with a friend and loved one. Think about the most wonderful vacation you have ever taken. Recall the moment of intense peace that you felt while viewing a spectacular sunset, or standing on the top of a glorious mountain. Remember experiencing the grandeur of nature and feeling yourself to be an important part of a greater whole.

During the process of this adventure that we are undertaking together, we begin to tap into the power of our peak experiences. We learn to shape and direct our lives on the path that we choose, the path of our heart's desire. We develop the mental and emotional mechanisms required to make these peak experiences commonplace. We learn to have peak experiences in areas of our lives where before we had only bleak experiences. We learn to make our work life and our dealings with others a series of fulfilling victories.

In order to regain the experience of these peak moments in our lives, let's practice recalling the situations and the feelings attached to them. When we return to those times of joy and wonder, we are again able to feel the magic of being alive. By carrying these feelings over into the present, we can energize ourselves to move toward positive changes in our lives now.

Peak Experience Visualization

Instructions:
- Allow 10 minutes for this exercise.
- Find a quiet place where you will not be disturbed.
- If you prefer, put on some soft, relaxing music.
- Settle back comfortably in your chair.
- Close your eyes and prepare to travel back to your own peak experiences.

1. Remember a particular incident in which you felt an enormous sense of joy and fulfillment. What was happening? Who was there? What was your accomplishment? Remember as many details as possible. What were the sights, sounds, smells?

2. Remember very clearly how it felt to you to be a part of this outstanding event. Look at your face: how do you look? Look at your body, your actions, and notice how they appear. Enjoy the sense of personal empowerment that you felt at that time.

3. Revel in this moment for a while. Enjoy the feelings. Notice how you feel not only emotionally but also mentally and physically. Do you feel clear and focused? Do you feel relaxed and strong? Notice all of your feelings.

4. Open your eyes and make note of those feelings. Record these responses so that you will remember what you are striving for and what is truly important to you.

5. Fold your hands and sit quietly for a moment. Then stretch and move around a little to refocus your energies for the day. Each time you feel alone or fearful, take a moment to fold your hands, sit quietly, tap into and anchor yourself in those feelings of strength and empowerment. Our job together in this book is to recreate those feelings of strength and personal control over our lives each and every day.

---

*There are no limitations to the mind
except those we acknowledge.*

Napoleon Hill

Releasing Yourself

We are all beings of mind, body and spirit, but most important is the spirit that is our inner core. Our spirit, or inner direction, tells us when we are on the right path, our own true way. Within spirit lies the wisdom that lets us know when we are following our own perfect design and speaking our own unique truth. From our spirit springs unconditional love not only for self but for others. Our spirit is the very best within each of us.

Mind is linked with ego. Ego was originally meant to serve our greater Purpose or design. Ego was meant to serve our inner, higher selves through the expression of our personal integrity in right action.

Somewhere along the line of our development as social beings, the ego became a force for alienation from others. We began to erect "ego defense mechanisms" in order to protect who we think we are from the scrutiny of others. We developed concepts like "not good enough" and "not able to."

Mind and ego need not be barriers or blocks to our fulfillment. When we understand that thoughts and actions are linked, we are able to use our minds and egos to accomplish the goals we set for our own fulfillment. We can learn to synchronize mind, body and spirit in order to develop and maintain balance in our lives. In this state, all of our capacities are under our control, including our thoughts, our actions and our beliefs. When we absolutely decide to take control of our lives, *without reservation*, we are open to our fullest potential.

Part of my life work is to go into corporations to train people to take control of their own lives. This includes taking responsibility for their successes and failures. I often get the response from trainees, "But *they* are doing it to us."

There will always be people who will not act the way they *should* act toward us. There will always be people who will not do their part of the job, who will not care about others, who are not trained to manage well or who are incompetent. Each time we blame our level of productivity, our ability to care for others, our attitudes and our success on what we are getting from others, we are acting as victims of life rather than as mature, capable adults. We all know that bad things do

---

I am the master of my fate.
I am the captain of my soul.

William Ernest Henley

happen to good people. The question is, do we learn and grow from the events of our lives, or do we moan and give up? The answer is, we grow.

How do we return to the harmony of perfectly integrated mind, body, and spirit? *We decide.* We do not allow negative self-image, damaging self-talk and low self-esteem to destroy our inner harmony. We refuse to allow bad habits, well-meaning friends and helpful enemies, or modeling from parents or peers, to become the ruling force in our thoughts. We are no longer bound by phrases like:

"I can't believe I said something that stupid."
"I'm not a very good parent."
"You know better than that."
"How could you be so stupid?"
"Why aren't you more like (your brother, your sister, your friend)?"
"That wasn't very smart."
"You don't really want to do thus-and-so."
"It would be such a disappointment to us after all we've done for you."

Just because you have practiced demeaning self-talk and limited faith in yourself in the past does not mean that you are required or forced to continue that behavior in the future. *The past only determines future behavior insofar as you allow it to do so!* Our lives are run by our own design, either consciously or unconsciously. We create ourselves through our decisions and actions. Of course, we do this within the context of the universal whole, of which we are a part.

Exercise
Your Favorite Place

This exercise is designed to allow you to neutralize the cares and woes of the day. You can release all excess tension and worry by taking yourself away to the most wonderful place in the world for you. It is your chance for a mini-vacation and a quick trip to futureland. It is an opportunity to discover that your mind does in fact respond to your direction.

We are in God as the wave is in the ocean.

Eric Butterworth

- Allow approximately 15 minutes for this exercise.
- Find a quiet place where you will not be disturbed.
- Settle back comfortably in your chair.
- Close your eyes and allow your body to relax as totally as you can.
- As you relax, fill all the spaces of your mind with a spectrum of colors. This releases all extraneous thoughts and images.

Begin by picturing the color blue. Allow the color blue to fill all of the spaces of your mind. Once you have filled your mind with the color blue, change the color to the color green allowing the color green to push all other images from your mind. Allow the color green to change to the color red as the color red fills all of the spaces of your mind. Relax into the color red and allow it to change to the color yellow, bright, warm relaxing yellow. Finally, allow the color white to fill your mind so that all other images or thoughts have been pushed out of your mind by the color white.

Once your mind is clear and relaxed, begin to imagine your favorite place. This is your special place. It could be a place that is real, that you have been to before or perhaps a place you want to go to.It could be a totally imaginary place, a place that only you have dreamed of, a place of peace and harmony and balance. A place of beauty and serenity that you personally have designed. This special place may be yours alone or it may be peopled with your loved ones. It may be indoors or outdoors, it may have walls and windows or only a floating roof to shade you from the sun. As you relax into this picture of your special place, notice the sights, the sounds, the special smells that make it yours. Enjoy this place and settle in; it belongs to you!

While in your special place, take a close look around. There may be things about your dreams that you never noticed before. There may be people whom you never expected to see in your favorite place. There may be aspects of your favorite place that begin to tell you what is important to you, what is most meaningful in your life.

Relax and enjoy this special place; you will return to it a number of times during our journey together. This place is your safe place, your place of wisdom, a place that holds many of the answers for your life.

Experiences

People have many varied experiences while doing this exercise. For example, I picture my retreat in the mountains. I picture all of the aspects that are important to me, the unique shape, the size, the colors, the furnishings and the landscaping. My retreat is surrounded by trees that hold their green and glorious color in all seasons. In the main room there is a large stone fireplace, a desktop computer, a comfortable leather couch, a wall of books, a painting and a Japanese vase. The floor is deeply carpeted in pale blue. The tones of the room are southwestern and soft. In the solarium there is a window seat lined with soft cushions. It is here that I read at night and write at sunrise. During the day, at times of renewal, I walk the path around the lake to energize myself. I experience a sense of total peace here.

Personal Power

We have the power to love ourselves enough to choose, at this very moment, to act in our own best interests. We can release ourselves for our own greater good, get out of our own way and achieve our highest purpose. No matter how much time has passed, no matter how weak our decision-making skills were before, the decision to act in accordance with our best possible selves is made in an instant.

The moment we choose to release ourselves from self-imposed bondage we begin to soar and to excel. We begin to have a sense of personal power, of purpose and of control over the events in our lives that make us happy or unhappy.

The body is our vehicle for action. It exists to carry out our purpose and to demonstrate our love for self and others. It is our instrument to actualize our thoughts and intentions. It is the dwelling place for our spirit and mind. As a responder, our body does exactly what the mind tells it to do. It can get cancer or cure it. It can run the five-minute mile or the "impossible" four-minute mile. It can warm us when we are cold or allow us to freeze to death. The body is neutral. It will respond exactly as the mind tells it to. Notice the next time you decide to change lanes while driving. Unless you are very attentive, the second you decide to move from one lane to another, the muscles in your hands are already turning the wheel. Once you have the picture in your mind, the body responds. We must be most attentive to the pictures we hold in our mind because that is exactly what we will find in our behavior.

Positive and Negative Imagery

The mind is the driving mechanism for the body. You create the life you envision in your mind. What you hold in your mind is drawn to you because you believe what you see. You then act on that belief and fulfill

---

Belief in limits creates limited people.

Dr. Georgi Lozanov

your own prophecy. We think that we think about what we get, but in actual fact, we get what we think about. To be successful with what we think, we want to train our minds to work for us.

These principles are applied successfully in every field of human endeavor. The United States Olympic Committee supports training in mental practice. Golf and tennis stars have written extensively about the "inner game" of their respective sports.

While in solitary confinement in a North Vietnamese POW camp known as the Hanoi Hilton, Air Force Colonel George Hall played an imaginary round of golf every day of his five-and-a-half year incarceration. He pictured each course he had ever played. He played each hole carefully, reading the greens, testing the wind, picturing the lie of each sand trap. He hit each ball and watched its course through the air and across the grass. He replaced each divot and acted totally in accordance with his normal behavior on the golf course. Less than one month after his release, Colonel Hall played in the New Orleans Open. He shot 76, his former four-stroke handicap!

Other prisoners have mentally practiced playing musical instruments, building or remodeling their homes, or playing professional or amateur sports. After their release, they are able to accomplish what they had practiced in their minds with the same level of skill they would have possessed had they actually been performing the task. The mind does not know the difference between a carefully crafted mental image energized by Passion, and the real thing. This is why what we put into our minds is so vitally important. There is no such thing as an idle thought.

When we picture an action in our mind, our fine muscles are activated and we are actually practicing what we picture. Dr. Richard Suinn, psychologist and researcher, states that "Soviet athletes make a career of competition, and they place a great deal of importance on the mind determining athletic success." Dr. Suinn developed a mind-training program for the 1976 U.S. Olympic ski team. The skiers practiced their ski runs in their imagination, mentally correcting errors and perfecting their skills. Charles Tickner, 1978 Olympic gold-medalist in figure skating, used relaxation and confidence-building statements every day.

Using the imagination for success is not a technique limited to athletes. The brilliant scientist and inventor Nikola Tesla used his

---

Achievement is the inevitable and natural by-product of awareness.

Timothy Gallwey, "The Inner Game of Tennis"

powers of visualization to formulate his ideas into reality. While watching a sunset one evening he "saw" the concept of "alternating" current, which was so superior to Thomas Edison's "direct" current method that it became the standard throughout the world. Tesla set up his generator to take advantage of the power of Niagara Falls, and ushered in the age of cheap, practical electricity. Tesla had trained his creative visualization capabilities to such a high degree that he was able to integrate details located in many different parts of his vast storehouse of knowledge.

Dr. Carl Simonton helps cancer patients at his treatment centers. His treatment is based on a combination of conventional medical care such as radiation therapy and the added advantage of mental self-healing. Norman Cousins, author of *Anatomy of an Illness*, is known as "the man who laughed himself well." Through a combination of traditional medical care, positive self-statements and high daily doses of laughter, he won back his health. Dr. Bernie Siegel has gained a national reputation from his books *Love, Medicine and Miracles* and *Peace, Love and Healing* which teach us how to love ourselves well.

There are numerous examples of outstanding business people who use mental imagery to be more successful. Charles Garfield, author of *Peak Performers: The New Heroes of American Business*, says, "In business, peak performers report using mental rehearsal for specific micro situations: presentations at board meetings, a sales encounter with a difficult customer, a speech to a large group. They may be unaware of using a formally defined skill. Few in our study were acquainted with the term mental rehearsal. I frequently hear responses like 'Yes, I imagine things in advance, sometimes over and over. But I never knew that had a name.' "

We frequently practice negative imagery without even realizing it. When we worry about what "might" happen, for instance, we may imagine disaster. When we live in the realms of "what if" and "if only I hadn't," we are using imagery to sustain our reality. When we put ourselves through the wringer of all the gruesome potential problems each day holds, we are using this technique most effectively. But in these cases we are using it to impede our own fulfillment.

> *Two men look out through the same bars*
> *One sees mud, and one sees stars.*
>
> William Wordsworth

The mind is capable of generating images of either accomplishment and greatness, or gloom and doom. We choose which set of possibilities we entertain.

The Eagle Visualization is designed to give us practice in directing our mental energy toward the positive aspects of life. It guides us into imagining what it feels like when we reach our highest levels of experience. When we practice this feeling we can recreate it any time we feel "down." The Eagle Visualization reminds us to fly.

Eagle Visualization

- Allow 10 minutes for this exercise.
- Go to a quiet place.
- Put on some quiet, relaxing music.
- Sink down comfortably in your chair.
- Close your eyes and breathe slowly, comfortably and deeply.

As you relax, let your mind wander to a time in your life that was great fun. What are you doing? Why is this activity fun? Look at your life. What sorts of things do you enjoy doing most? What gives you the greatest   pleasure?

Now let your mind soar. If you could be anything or do anything in your life, what would it be? What would you look like, feel like, be like? Remember that there are no restrictions. This image belongs to you alone, and there are no limits.

As your mind soars, begin to imagine yourself as an eagle. Let your mind turn into the image of an eagle. Leave your physical body and allow your eagle mind to circle above the earth, flying higher and higher and higher with each circle. As you look down on the turning earth from this great height, notice that time seems to stand still. Then it starts to move backward. As you watch the world turn, see the panorama of your life displayed in front of you like a moving picture. As you watch, detached, notice that time has moved backwards to the day of your birth!

You are fascinated but emotionally detached. The observation of your life is interesting and informative. Starting with your birth, the years begin to move forward again. Your years pass in front of you from infancy to childhood, childhood to youth, youth to adulthood.

As the story of your life unfolds to the present time, notice that there is a scene you do not recognize immediately. Focus your eagle eyes and begin to see your future. The picture fills out to include the activities, people and possessions that are important to you in your unlimited vision above. Observing your future from this great height, you realize how complete you are and how possible it is to achieve all that you want. Continue to relax as you open your eyes and record what you discovered you want to be. Record what you found in the area below or in a personal journal.

Personal Journal

A personal journal is a record of the things that you learn, know or do each day. It can be a spiral notebook or a very sophisticated and expensive diary. The choice of the type of journal is yours, but whatever kind of book you choose, it is important that you record what you learn each day. You may want to record the ideas and thoughts that come to you in that twilight time before sleep. You may pick up good ideas and insights from conversations, books, television, your place of worship and other people.

When we attempt to remember an important idea without recording it, we often forget the essence of the concept and then cannot draw on it when we want to. When we record what we learn, know and do, we can review these ideas and concepts at any time without having to "try" to remember. When we record information, we have it available to us more readily and without the confusion of "hindsight" interpretation. If you have ever had an argument with someone over what was said in a past conversation you will have already experienced the value of writing things down! Our minds can follow our inner guidance much more easily when we pay close attention to the information that we are given.

Letting Go to Power

Great power exists in the process of letting go of "should" and "have to." It comes from understanding who we are, and why we are here. Personal power springs from the intense, alive energy that exists in every cell of our bodies. Our experience of personal power is especially vivid during the peak experiences we considered a little while ago. In those moments of truest living, we have more than red and white corpuscles circulating in our bloodstream. We have huge hidden reserves of energy and creativity.

And alone and without his nest shall the eagle fly across the sun.

Kahlil Gibran

We tap into this available reservoir only when we feel joyful, when we are doing what we love to do. Personal power is the energy that we feel when we leave a job we tolerate in order to do something "fun." This power exists day after day, hour after hour, moment by moment, and is available to us always. We become our own worst enemy when we disinherit ourselves from what should naturally be ours, being the great creative beings that we are. To be our great selves, it is necessary that we make the decision to claim the best every day, with every event of our lives. We are not meant to be excluded from the joy that is within us. It can be ours in each experience of our life if we will only choose it. The choice is for life!

When I came close to death in a sky-diving accident I made the ultimate decision to be fully alive as long as I live. Others have learned this important lesson along the way. Charles Garfield has researched the lives of people who seek fulfillment in their lives. Some of these stories provide fascinating insight into the inextricable link between Passion and work.

Joseph Weider and his brother Benjamin started with no money and little education. What they did have was a profound understanding of fitness and peak health, plus a desire to share their knowledge. Step by step, their total commitment to their Purpose has produced results for millions of Americans. They have published magazines, designed bodybuilding equipment, and started exercise programs for women, children and senior citizens. Their vision has motivated other people to improve themselves.

Beth Milwid, although a Phi Beta Kappa from Stanford and holder of a master's degree, felt that she was blocked from moving beyond middle-level responsibility in business because she was a woman. Fortunately for her, she was more interested in having her success than her excuses. She went back to school and got her Ph.D. in psychology and finished a post-doctoral business program at the UCLA Graduate School of Management. She then became manager of career development at Crocker Bank in San Francisco.

Beth then decided to accomplish her Purpose of moving women up the corporate ladder by working with the prevailing forces rather than against them. She left the bank to form her own company, Life Works.

The mind is its own place, and in itself
Can make a heaven of a hell, a hell of a heaven.

John Milton

The purpose of Life Works is to understand the dynamics of organizations, in order to help women gain major corporate responsibilities.

Psychologist Brandon Hall joined the Wilson Learning Corporation of Eden Prairie, Minnesota, in 1981. His goal was to successfully recommend Wilson Learning management training programs to his corporate clients in Silicon Valley. His first nine months were a struggle and life was not comfortable. Dr. Hall worked on his own self-confidence by being willing to hear "no" and yet move on. He developed a practice of analyzing problem situations within potential client companies on a "macro," or large-scale, level and suggesting specific solutions down through a "micro," or detailed, view. He used positive self-talk to prepare his mind for interactions with these possible clients in advance. In 1983 he made his first million dollars in sales in a single year. Dr. Hall's belief in himself helped him keep on trying. He knew that a sense of personal fulfillment fuels success.

When Dr. Garfield was asked what the peak performers in his study said that the rest of us could learn, he answered: "They said something I didn't understand at the beginning. They'd say, 'Sometimes I ask myself, if I only had one hour to live, what would be so important to me that I'd be thinking about it during my last hour on earth?' It turned out they only talked about two things. They talked about work. They were particularly proud of work, as yet unfinished, that made an impact—what we're calling work with a mission. Not one of those people ever said, 'With an hour left to live, I thought of my mutual fund.' Nobody mentioned possessions of any kind. They talked about love and they talked about work."

Life without fulfillment is life driven by anxiety, frustration and unhappiness. The alternative is for you to know that a life of fulfillment of your deepest Purpose is available to you. Life with fulfillment is life filled with joy, interest, energy and the thrill of success.

The Bond of Being Human

We are not alone in making this choice. We are all in this together and we are all here for one primary purpose, to make the world a better place to live. When life isn't running along a smooth path and "things"

What lies behind us and what lies before us are small matters compared to what lies within us.

Ralph Waldo Emerson

don't seem to be going our way, we can feel isolated, miserable and without hope. Not realizing that we have chosen our unhappy state and allowed our life to be out of order, we retreat from oneness with the whole of life and all other human beings around us, aloof in our misery. The attitude is: "No one has it quite as hard as I do. No one really understands how difficult it is for me. Why can't I make things work the way I want them to?" We separate ourselves from our support group, our friends, family, close acquaintances. This cuts us off from one of our greatest sources of power: the spiritual bond that exists with all other humans.

The power of the universe flows through all of us, animating our spirit and filling our being. When we move with this flow, releasing our personal power to achieving our highest and best, we automatically empower others who are also working for their highest purpose. We are not alone! We are part of a network of invisible strands that connect all individuals who are in tune with this universal energy.

For each choice we make that holds us back, limits us, makes us unhappy, we are also holding others back by diminishing the flow that connects all of us. The universe is abundant and willing to give; only the mind of man can stop the flow.

Charles Wedemeyer is the assistant coach of football at Los Gatos High School in California. Coach Wedemeyer uses football as a metaphor for life, honor and growth. He teaches his team about Pride and Heart: Pride in oneself and Heart for others. Charles Wedemeyer feels that those two aspects of humanity are what makes each of us the very best that we can be. As the former head coach of Los Gatos High School, Charles Wedemeyer brought his team from the bottom of the league to the state championships. They accomplished this not just by what Coach Wedemeyer taught them about football, but by what he taught them about life.

Charles Wedemeyer has Lou Gehrig's disease. This is a disease that attacks the muscles until the individuals cannot walk, use their hands or even breathe on their own. Because of a tracheotomy performed to save his life, Charles Wedemeyer cannot even speak. He talks with the help of his wife, Lucy Wedemeyer. She reads his lips and speaks for him. None of these disabilities has stopped Charles Wedemeyer from teaching us about courage, about purpose and about

---

Winning is not the only thing.
Living and striving whether you win or lose is the only thing.

Charles Wedemeyer

passion for life. Even with this crippling disease, Coach Wedemeyer stays on the job, doing what he most loves to do in life.

Finding Your Purpose, Passion and Path

Purpose is our overall reason for being.

Passion is what we do in demonstration of that Purpose, generally the work we do.

Our **Path** is the way or road we take to fulfill our Purpose. Power comes from being willing to take the risk to live our Passion and our Purpose and to follow our Path. As we journey through this book we explore our inner selves to find what brings us inner peace and joy, our pointers toward the greater meaning of our lives. The journey is at once thrilling, painful, exciting, humorous, interesting and challenging. On this journey we discover our own value, and learn to express that value in the lives we create.

Finding the Great Creative You consists of seven adventure steps to accomplish the goal of finding our Purpose, Passion and Path.

Adventure Step One: THE ESSENCE OF YOU

In this step we explore who we really are, beyond the social self that we present, presumably for our own protection, to others every day. Our real self is our finest essence, the magic that we share with very trusted friends at very special times. This is our opportunity to let that person out forever and to feel safe doing so.

Adventure Step Two: FINDING YOUR LIFE'S MISSION

Each of us has an overriding Purpose for being here. This step helps to identify what that Purpose is and how we can begin to demonstrate it. We discover our highest visions beyond mere survival.

Adventure Step Three: DUMPING YOUR BLOCKS

We all have blocks that prevent us from being the best that we can and doing the best that we can. This step gives us specific methods to move past those blocks.

Adventure Step Four: THE POWER OF FOCUS

The power of any opportunity or desire comes from the ability to focus on what we want and put all of our energy in that direction.

Adventure Step Five: THE DECISION TO ACT

All the best intentions in the world fall by the wayside when an idea is not strengthened by the decision to act. This step commits us to moving in the right direction

Adventure Step Six: LIVING YOUR VISION

This step provides training and practice in the skills of mental visioning and affirmation. As we think, so we behave.

Adventure Step Seven: THE ACTION PLAN

This is where the plan comes together. Without a specific plan to put into action, we will end up where we started. This step moves us decisively in the right direction.

The Pathwalkers: PEOPLE WHO LIVE THEIR PASSION

On our journey we will also talk to people we call Pathwalkers. Pathwalkers are people who have discovered their Purpose and their Passion. We will find out how they found their great creativity. Let's start with Dr. Ken Blanchard, co-author of *The One Minute Manager*.

Pathwalker: Ken Blanchard

Dr. Kenneth Blanchard has profoundly affected the day-to-day, bottom-line management style of America's corporations with a unique approach to Human Resources Development. Everything from the Fortune 500 organization to the entrepreneurial enterprise has benefited from his innovative thinking in *The One Minute Manager* library. The collected works in this series have now sold more than 7 million copies, and have been translated into more than 20 languages. Dr. Blanchard's newest book, *The Power of Ethical Management*, is co-authored with Dr. Norman Vincent Peale.

Expressing Purpose in Every Relationship

"While working with Norman Vincent Peale on *The Power of Ethical Management*, I started to see the difference between a purpose and a goal. I think a goal is something to be accomplished and a purpose is something that is ongoing; kind of like the road you travel on through life, while goals are stops along the way.

"My first attempt to even deal with Purpose was a number of years ago when I made a tape for my own funeral. I decided that I didn't want to leave it to a minister to try to say the things I wanted to say. I was really influenced by the story of the founder of the Nobel Peace Prize, Alfred Nobel, whose brother was killed in World War I. When Alfred went to read the obituary in the local Swedish newspaper, he found they had gotten him and his brother mixed up and the obituary was his own. The obituary was all about this man who had created this destructive material. Many people don't realize that Alfred Nobel invented dynamite, which could be used to destroy nature. He didn't like that description, so he asked, 'How can I be remembered for something else?' Friends advised him to start something that stood for the opposite of destruction.

"When I first started working on my own purpose, I thought I would be able to come up with a snappy statement like a mission statement for an organization: that my life was about service and love and so on. I realized, in trying to think of one single statement, that I really needed several to cover all the different relationships in my life. I was on a program once with Tom Landry, who is the only coach the Dallas Cowboys have ever had. Now, Landry's a very, very calm person.

"The host asked him how he could stay so calm in the midst of a crazy game like professional football. Landry's response was quick and to the point. He said, 'It's easy for me to stay calm, I have my priorities in order. First comes the Lord. Second comes my wife. Third come my children, and fourth comes my job. If I lose on Sunday I have a lot left over. A lot of people lose on Sunday and they have nothing left over because they think life is all about winning.'

"I went about writing a purpose statement for the different roles I have in my life. Norman Vincent Peale came along at a time when I needed someone to help me deal with some of my spiritual questions and issues. My spiritual purpose is to live a good Christian life, exemplifying the principles that Jesus taught. That's something you can accomplish any given day. What you need to do is be consciously aware of it so you could have a goal of reading the Bible, or doing something positive. In an article about writing a mission statement, Richard Bolles, who wrote *What Color Is Your Parachute,* said that you can't think of purpose and mission without spirituality. I think that is important.

"My greatest joy in life is the relationships that I have developed with my wife Margie, my kids, with friends, and with all the people in my company. After all, how many people on their deathbeds say, 'I wish I had worked harder?' They all say they wish they had loved more, and cared more, and laughed more. I try to be with people when they need me and recognize that we're all on this planet trying to figure out the journey. None of us can do it alone; we need each other.

"In my role as a husband, my purpose is to be a good husband to Margie: helping, supporting and encouraging her in her life's ambitions. What is my role as a father? To be a loving, caring father who helps my kids and encourages them as they journey through life. That's also true of my mom and Margie's mom.

"Purpose statements are your general mission, what are you doing? What is my role as a friend? To be a caring, loving friend and to help support my friends in their goals and journey through life. What is my purpose as a writer? To get the 'b.s.' out of the behavioral sciences and make principles come alive for people so they can use the information in their everyday lives.

"What is my Purpose as an entrepreneur? I ought to be the 'soul' of the company. I was in Japan a few years ago and met the chairman of the board of one of the major companies over there. Somebody asked what his purpose was. He said, 'To be soul.' Through him the values of the company pass. His job was to wander around and affirm those values. That is a nice kind of purpose statement.

"The big picture is that my purpose in life is caring for and loving others and supporting them on life's journey. My work is helping others, practicing my spiritual beliefs and living the kind of life exemplified in the teachings of the Bible."

Staying on Track

"We waver from our purpose when we let our egos get in the way; when we start to get into win-lose confrontations; when we want to look good. I've had my moments when I couldn't see the forest for the trees and got caught up in 'being right' or 'being in charge.' The biggest thing that gets me back on track is Margie and the great people around me who won't let me get away with it. When I start getting a big head or believing my own press, they bring me back to reality.

"I am really conscious right now of starting my day more slowly. We all have two selves: an inner self that is reflective and thoughtful and an external, task-oriented self that is used to getting jobs done. The problem is that it takes much longer to wake up your inner self than your external task-oriented self. Most of us wake up in the morning and leap into our task-oriented self, running around, trying to eat at the same time we're washing. We have phones in our cars so we can talk at the same time that we're driving. We race around so much that we don't wake up that inner self.

"I've been making sure I have an hour and a half or so before I have to do anything, so I can enter my day more slowly. I start off reading excerpts from the Bible, a wonderful book called *The Promise of a New Day* and the *Daily Word*, which my mom has sent me for years. I've been trying to walk or do some other exercise, and have quiet time to enter the day more slowly to keep on track. This causes you to be clearer about purpose. You can also get your pride out of the way, become more patient and persistent, and get things in perspective. This time gives you the capacity to step outside what you are doing and see it from a distance.

"Don't race around before you have a chance to think about what your day is for. That is the greatest way to find the creative abilities inside. Recognize that working on your purpose is an ongoing lifetime process, something you are continually examining. Your goal is eventual inner peace. That is the key element in life."

ADVENTURE

1

STEP

The Essence of You

Who you are is expressed in *what you do*. What we do shows our essential self, our true being. Our actions and behavior manifest our basic belief systems. How we act demonstrates our view of life and our commitment to life. Who we are is determined by specific influences:

- our initial birth plan
- our learning history
- our positive or negative self-talk
- our powerful traumatic and positive experiences
- our strength of character

Each of these aspects of our lives shapes who we are, how we view the world and how we make decisions. Each influence directs our lives along certain pathways. Each one serves to guide the direction of our lives as it influences our choices.

Although we are strongly influenced by the experiences of our lives and the things that we are taught, we can override any information previously ingrained when we consciously choose to do so. As we investigate each area in more detail, we begin to see the influence of our past learning. We learn how to change our minds, our patterns, and our lives.

Everything that is, is within.

Anonymous

Initial Birth Plan

Your **initial birth plan** is your genetic heritage. It includes all of those behaviors and habits that are a part of your genetically programmed nature. Some of us are born active, assertive, creative or outgoing. Others are born quiet, easygoing, sensitive and artistic. There are as many combinations of traits as there are people. Our nature is a starting point, a beginning. It is what we do with what we are born with that is most important.

Learning History

Your **learning history** includes all of the information you have been taught. It includes the things your parents taught you, like how to behave and what is right and wrong. It includes your belief systems like religion, morals, ethics and beliefs about success and failure. It includes all that you learned in school. It includes everything you learned from your friends, peers and colleagues. It includes all that you have seen and heard and all that you *believe* that you have seen and heard. You are shaped by your perceptions, the views that you take of the world.

Positive and Negative Self-Talk

Our **positive and negative self-talk** is a strong guiding force in our lives. Our self-talk is composed of those inner dialogues that we have with ourselves around situations–those mini-scenarios with which we create an entire inner world. Self-talk includes our *reviewing* of the little stories that happened previously, as well as *previewing* stories that we fear or hope will happen. It includes stories that have no basis at all in reality, which we create from our strongest emotions, love and fear.

Have you ever become upset over something and then found out that it wasn't true? Have you ever waited for a person who was late for an appointment or a friend who was late coming home? While you waited, maybe you got angry because you felt personally abused or discounted. You may have judged the individual unprofessional. Perhaps you were worried because your friend might have been hurt. When the person arrived you finally got a factual explanation. Perhaps they had a flat tire, or they had been caught in traffic. Yet while you waited you created a reality all your own, a story based on fear and anxiety. You created this inner story based on the things that you were telling yourself, your self-talk.

Our inner reality, our self-talk, shapes our behavior and shapes and reshapes our belief systems. One way to open ourselves to the inner eye, the eye of truth that sees us as we really are, is to take a look at our self-talk.

We are capable of generating our reality without another person to interact with. We make up stories about how things are, or were, or should be. We can get angry, disappointed or scared when we forget to see the whole picture or elicit the other person's point of view. Sometimes we jump first and ask questions later. Some of us have a tendency to put ourselves down or "catastrophize." We even say things like, "I'm such a jerk," or "How could I have been so dumb," or "I don't have what it takes."

Becoming conscious of and taking control of this inner language is vital to our well-being. I have found a wonderful little question that helps me focus on the reality of the situation when negative self-talk pulls me off base. The question is, "Is it really true?" Is it really true that I am a jerk, or dumb, or that I don't have what it takes? No! It is not true. This question helps us to stop and investigate what we are saying; it helps us to become conscious of our internal dialogue. When we say negative things to ourselves we develop a negative belief system. Then we begin to live as if those negative pictures were true. The stories in this book of the Pathwalkers, people who have guided their own lives, prove that *we all have what it takes.* We just need faith in ourselves, some personal planning, and most especially the *willingness to use what we know.*

When psychologists work with people who want to fulfill their lives and self-actualize, or with those who have emotional blocks, the most important aspect of behavior they must deal with is the person's self-talk. I used to say that I was not a very assertive person. I created a certain view of myself and then lived by certain rules. The truth is, however, that I am just as assertive as I choose to be.

We need to develop the concept, "I *can* do whatever I *choose* to do." Many public speakers and actors are very shy in their private lives. But instead of dwelling on the limitation "I am shy, so I can't," they focus on "I can, I know how to, so I am able to." They become outgoing and assertive through practice. I grew from being a "shy" person to working as a public speaker and corporate trainer. It took many steps to get to my goal. I went from assertiveness training courses to public speaking courses to accepting many speaking opportunities in front of social and civic groups. *Being willing to grow and learn is the key.*

The following exercise helps you change your self-talk from a detrimental influence to a resource. When you change your self-talk, you strengthen the power of your mind to motivate rather than block.

Exercise
Self-Talk Awareness

- Find a quiet place where you will be undisturbed.
- Make a list of all the little nasty and fearful things you say about yourself in the different areas of your life.

Examples are given with each area, to give you an idea of the kinds of dialogue to look for. Examine the following areas:

Work Relationships
Personal Relationships
Parents
Children
Money
Sports
Body Image

Nasty little sayings: Work Relationships
I will never get this project done!
I hate this job.
My boss is an idiot and I am self-employed.
Nobody appreciates me here.

Your list:

_____

_____

_____

_____

Nasty little sayings: Personal Relationships.
I will never find a fulfilling relationship on this planet.
My spouse doesn't understand me.
I am too (fat, ugly, old, thin, tall, short) to find a loving relationship.
I want the perfect relationship with no problems.

Your list:

_____

_____

_____

_____

Nasty little sayings: Parents.
  My parents tell everyone that they had no children.
  Why weren't my parents rich?
  My parents never really loved me, so what can you expect from me?
  My parents were so strict that I never learned how to socialize.
  My father had no ambition, so I can't succeed.

Your list:

_____

_____

_____

_____

Nasty little sayings: Children
  Of all the kids in the world why did I get this one?
  I was definitely not cut out to be a parent.
  Where in the world did these brats come from?
  Won't this kid ever shut up!
  I cannot handle teenagers; it's time to give them away.

Your list:

_____

_____

_____

_____

Nasty little sayings: Money
   I am not earning what I am worth.
   Nobody could live on what I am earning!
   I am stuck in a financial rut and the world is running over me.
   If I'm so smart, how come I'm not rich?

Your list:

_____

_____

_____

_____

Nasty little sayings: Sports and Physical Activities
   I am such a klutz.
   I am always the last one chosen for the team.
   I am a lousy (golf, tennis, volleyball, baseball, football) player.
   I am really out of shape.
   The only thing I excel at is being an Olympic-class couch potato.

Your list:

_____

_____

_____

_____

Nasty little sayings: Body Image
   I am too (fat, skinny, mediocre).
   I have truly gangly legs.
   My hair is (a dustmop, scraggly, nonexistent).
   I have a truly wonderful body, it's a wonder that anyone could look
like this!

Your list:

_____

_____

_____

_____

Besides saying nasty little things to ourselves in general, we often make impossible comparisons between ourselves and other people. The comparisons are impossible because we can never *be* anyone other than who we are. Someone may say, "I would like to sing, but I don't sound like Julie Andrews." Well, neither does Judy Collins, Linda Ronstadt or Carly Simon. Each singer sounds completely different from the other and each one is unique. Who in the world sounds like Pavarotti but himself? That is what makes him special.

We frequently compare our worst points with someone else's best points, for example, "My legs are short and fat, not like Ann's—which are long and thin," "My hairline is receding, not like Sam's, which is thick and luxurious." This is a no-win situation. These comparisons ignore the fact that Ann of the beautiful legs may not feel very lovely either, or that Sam's fine head of hair covers a brain loaded with learned inadequacies.

Instead, we can accept the fact that we are who we are and we look like what we look like. We can, of course, change what we look like. But the truly significant change is to change what we *feel like*. The way we do this is to accept ourselves and put energy into that acceptance. These exercises are designed to help in that process.

Nasty little sayings: Comparisons with Other People.
If I were tall like him I'd be much more successful.
If I were as beautiful as she is I'd have the world at my fingertips.
If I were as thin as Oprah I would try my luck in show business.
If I had the education she has I could be the boss too.
If I had the luck he has I wouldn't be where I am today.

Your list:

_____

_____

_____

_____

How do you feel after making these wonderful lists?
Is there a bridge nearby to jump off?
Why bother going on at all?
Nothing I do really seems to work.
I feel awful/terrible/wimpy/stupid/ineffective/impotent/ugly or generally not good.

Your list:

_____

_____

_____

_____

When we allow this kind of internal dialogue to fill our minds, it produces an ongoing low-level depression. It saps our energy and prevents us from achieving anything worthwhile with the circumstances we have before us right now. But the good news is: *our self-talk is not unalterably programmed into us; we can change it any time we choose.* Now is the time to either neutralize the above statements by asking if they are really true, or turn them into positive statements based on fact. Here are some examples of positive or self-enhancing statements. Write your own statements on the lines below.

Self-Embracing Statements: Work Relationships
I will get this job done and done well too!
I love working for myself and I do good work.
I am well appreciated here.

Your list:

_____

_____

_____

_____

Self-Embracing Statements: Personal Relationships.
I can find a meaningful relationship if I simply open myself to the possibility.
My spouse loves and cares for me.
I am perfect for a loving relationship.

Your list:

_____

_____

_____

_____

Self-Embracing Statements: Parents.
I am an adult now and can no longer blame my parents for my behavior. Not only that, I actually like being responsible.
My parents love me very much and I love them.
My parents did as well as they knew how.

Your list:

_____

_____

_____

_____

Self-Embracing Statements: Children
When I relax I really enjoy my children and watching them grow.
These children came from me and I love them.
I have been honored to hold an angel in my arms.

Your list:

_____

_____

_____

_____

Self-Embracing Statements: Money
I am capable and competent.
I will do what I love to do and the universe will provide the appropriate income.
I know how to manage my finances and meet my needs.

Your list:

_____

_____

_____

_____

Self-Embracing Statements: Sports and Physical Activities
I enjoy playing sports and doing physical things.
I am pretty good at (name your game).
I can easily get in shape with a little discipline.

Your list:

_____

_____

_____

_____

Self-Embracing Statements: Body Image
I am (gorgeous, handsome, wonderful).
I am most content with my looks.
As I face the mirror I see through the eyes of love for myself as well as others.

Your list:

_____

_____

_____

_____

Self-Embracing Statements: Comparisons with Other People.
I am perfectly fine as I am.
I am a whole person and I need compare myself to no one.
I am uniquely and wonderfully me.

Your list:

_____

_____

_____

_____

How do you feel after making *these* wonderful lists?
I feel that life is well worth living!
I feel marvelous.
Everything's coming up orchids.

Your list:

_____

_____

_____

How do you feel now after changing your self-talk?
I feel fantastic!
I feel more relaxed.
I feel excited and exciting.
I feel wonderful.
I feel empowered.

Your list:

_____

_____

_____

_____

_____

Stop-Think

There is a distinct possibility that with all of the practice you have had with nasty little sayings–years' and years' and years' worth!–that negative self-talk is still stronger than positive self-talk.

A powerful way to catch ourselves when we are making negative statements is a technique called **stop-think.** If we notice when we are about to beat ourselves up, we can replace those nasty little sayings with positive self-statements.

1. Each time you catch yourself making a negative statement immediately yell STOP in your mind and picture a large red stop sign. By doing this you have set up an incompatible behavior. You cannot think two thoughts at the same time.

2. Once you have got your mind's attention, clear it of the negative statement and immediately replace it with a Self-Embracing Statement. Repeat the positive statement several times, and also give yourself a physical cue. Fold your hands or touch your shoulder, or rest your hands gently on your hips. The physical action serves as a reminder that you like yourself and that you are worthy.

3. Do this each time you catch yourself thinking or saying negative statements. There is no time limit on feeling good. Use the stop-think technique every time throughout the day that you catch yourself being negative or hurtful. It is also useful when you catch yourself being negative about someone else.

No one can make me feel inferior without my consent.

Eleanor Roosevelt

Go back to your list of negative self-talk and select the negative phrase you use most often. For example, at work perhaps you grind your teeth and say at least 100 times a day, "If it weren't for that idiot who pretends to be my boss, I would be president of this company."

Now find the Self-Embracing Statement that is the counterpart to this negative statement. For example, "My boss is my boss and I am me. I am responsible for my behavior and my future." Write down this positive statement in large capital letters and anchor this thought by folding your hands or touching your chin or using whatever action is comfortable for you.

Your supreme Self-Embracing Statement:

_____

_____

_____

_____

Whenever you find yourself about to say something negative, counter it by stating something positive. In addition, write your Self-Embracing Statement on a separate piece of paper or a card. Put it where you are likely to notice it frequently—for example, on your bathroom mirror, your refrigerator, your car dashboard or in your wallet. This constant reinforcement of the positive over the negative will eventually replace the negative self-statement permanently. You will have taken control of your life and changed your mental programming.

Experiences

Here are some comments by people who have completed this exercise:

"Writing down my nasty little sayings helped me to uncover thoughts I wasn't aware of. So many were so unrealistic–therefore my expectations were often frustrated. I felt energized when I used the Self-Embracing Statements."

"I had a lot of difficulty doing this one at first as I found my very powerful negative images intruding in the form of questions like: 'Why are you bothering with this? You know it won't *really* change anything!' I had to go back several times to the Self-Embracing Statements and 'reset' my mind."

"For years I have prided myself on the fact that I am aware of my self-talk and always try to keep it under control. So I was fairly certain that my self-talk was basically clean of any negative feedback. Not so! At the completion of all of the exercises, I became alarmingly aware of little, petty negative conversations bouncing around in my sub-conscious mind. The way you developed your sequence and the examples you used were useful tools to jog my mind to think about potential negatives. The negatives were there and it was clear that I had to get them out!"

You can see from these comments that when we have practiced years of negative thinking, it may be difficult at first to let go of the negative and enjoy the positive. The negative is stronger only because we have spent so many years *practicing* the negative. We need to give life a chance!

There are many techniques to help us free our minds. The next exercise gives power and credibility to positive self-talk and takes us on a journey to our beginnings.

Guided Meditation
A Journey to Beginnings

- Allow at least 15 minutes for this exercise.
- Go to your quiet place and settle down comfortably.
- Breathe slowly, deeply and comfortably.

Begin by picturing a series of colors in order to clear your mind of all extraneous thoughts. Start with the color blue. Fill your mind with the color blue until it fills all the spaces. Slowly replace the color blue with the healing color green. Allow the color green to fade to the color yellow and once your mind is filled with the color yellow, fade that to the color white. Once your mind is clear and relaxed, return to your favorite place, the special place you created in your mind in the previous guided meditation.

In your favorite place find a small niche that calls to you. It may be a corner, a comfortable group of pillows, a pile of soft leaves, a hollow in the ground surrounded by flowers or a soft spot under a tree. This is your nesting place.

Lie down in your nesting place and allow your body and your mind to be at peace as you notice the gentle feeling you get while resting here and settling in.

Allow your mind to drift backwards in time as you picture yourself as a younger person. Remember falling in love, getting married, having a child. See yourself as a teenager, remember your first love, your first football game, your first driver's license. Remember yourself as a child, Envision yourself going to school for the first time, see yourself playing games with your friends, visualize yourself eating ice cream on a hot summer's day. And finally, see yourself as an infant. Envision yourself being amazed at life, watch yourself learning to walk. Enjoy these moments. Don't rush them. Relive your life in a gentle, easy way.

Allow a white cloud to fill your mind, soft and embracing. This cloud gently embraces your infant-self. Look into your peaceful, innocent baby face.

Release your infant self into the cloud and watch it disappear. Your infant self is now unborn. You are in your mother's womb, safe and protected, full of the potential of your life.

Release the small self that is you waiting for birth and drift further back in time. The potentiality that is you is now a white light waiting to enter the life process. Look down at the earth from a great height and see the earth through innocent eyes. Notice the amount of good on the earth and how it far exceeds the amount of evil. Notice the caring that the majority of people exhibit for each other. See all human beings with an individual beam of light in them, a beam of light similar to the one that you are now. See this beam of light filling each person.

Notice the sense of total peace in your existence. Hear the quiet of a life without "shoulds" and "woulds" and hurts. Notice the gentle look of the earth from so far above. See the earth as the astronauts do.

Notice how it feels to be free of self-judgment and free of the judgment of others. You are clear of all restrictions, negative learning, pain, suffering and anxiety. Your lightness is part of your recognition of your own light, which will stay with you eternally.

You are perfect as you are. You have chosen to be born and to live a life to serve your greater Purpose. Your Purpose is yours and yours alone. Only you can fulfill this Purpose. It is your gift to life—to your life and to the life of the planet. It is grand in its design and fits the greater

Change your thinking and you change your life.

Ernest Holmes

Purpose of all humanity. It may be to serve one minute only or to serve a lifetime. You are Amadeus, you are Einstein, you are Joe and you are Mary—all are equally unique, valuable and needed.

Love this person dearly, the person you are meant to be.

Move forward now toward the present, move through time. See yourself moving toward birth, being born, becoming a child, growing to a young adult, an adult, and finally see yourself as you are today—with one major difference. Today you are free of negative programming! You know, deeply know, yourself to be the light.

See yourself back in your nest in your favorite place. You are free of pain, alive, powerful, energized and perfect.

Return from your favorite place to the room where you started. Take with you the complete sense of personal knowing that you are whole and complete, that you are just as you were meant to be. Know that you can relax and live your life without fear and without judgment.

Keep this scene sacred in your mind and heart. You may recall these glorious moments anytime you choose to. As you do, you remember who you are and why you are here.

When we invest in monitoring and changing our self-talk we tap the most powerful resource that we have available to us. One woman who did this exercise commented, "I found this to be very powerful for I had neglected my child-self. Holding my child-self brought tears of love and recognition forth and gave me a sense of new beginnings." As you work through the exercises in this book you will become more and more capable of empowering yourself to do what you want to do with your life.

Let's invest some more time in using this asset to move us toward positive changes. The exercise below is designed to release us from the power of our negative images and replace them with images and ideas that work for us and give us strength. Many of us have been practicing imagery for years without giving it a name. When I ask the people I teach if they use imagery, most say, "No, not me." But when I ask them if they worry or are able to picture the worst thing that could happen, they always say, "Yes, of course!" We use imagery all of the time—we simply use it to help us fail rather than to help us succeed. The skills in this chapter teach us to use our imagery to help us grow and succeed rather than hurt and inhibit ourselves. Our strength comes from the power of our minds and the clarity of our thoughts.

Before you begin, have your personal journal handy, and something to write with. There is also blank space below the exercise in case you plan to use this book instead of a journal.

Exercise
Self-Talk and Mind Power

Find a quiet place where you will be undisturbed. Relax and clear your mind by picturing a series of colors. Start with the color blue. Let your whole mind be filled with the color blue. See it gently spread out into all the corners of your awareness, soothing everything it touches.

Now see this blue color slowly changing into the color green. Enjoy the healing touch of green for a few moments. If distracting thoughts enter your mind, allow them to be gently absorbed into the green that fills your whole mind.

Now see the green softly changing into the color red and finally the color yellow.

With your eyes still closed, monitor your body by scanning it from head to toe. As your awareness rests on each part of your body, relax the muscles in that part thoroughly. Feel the tension leave them. Check your forehead, your facial muscles, your neck and shoulders, your upper back, your lower back, your chest and stomach, your hips, thighs, legs and feet. As you check these muscle groups make certain that the muscles are smooth and free of pain or knots. Picture each muscle group as smooth and comfortable. Check to make certain that you have released all excess tension from your body.

Now, with your body and mind totally relaxed, begin to picture any scene that causes you difficulty or discomfort. It may be a worry scene where you imagine that you will fail at what you are attempting; it might be a disaster scene where you want to sky-dive but you picture yourself in an accident; it might be a financial disaster scene where you picture yourself with a warehouse full of product and no buyers; it may be a counseling service with no clients in the waiting room; it might be a heartbreaking scene in which the one you love leaves you for someone else or says no to your proposal of marriage. It could be any scene that you have consciously or unconsciously been practicing in your mind.

Fill in all of the details of the picture. If it is the sky-diving scene, picture yourself going splat on the ground after your chute fails to open. If it is the counseling service with no clients in the waiting room, picture yourself beginning to panic and picture your financial statement in the red. Picture your house payment overdue and your credit cards full. Really get the feel of it.

Once you have the scene very clearly pictured in your mind, picture the scene turning to smoke and disappearing. Allow the scene to fade from your awareness as you clear your mind. Picture a white light taking its place. Take your time. If the scene appears again, simply relax your body and again imagine the scene turning to smoke and *disappearing from your consciousness. Take a moment to monitor your body. Make sure that your muscles are relaxed and that your mind is truly clear.*

At this point we will replace the negative scene with a scene that will reinforce the positive outcome of your desires. Consider well what outcome you desire. (Later you will record this information in this book or in your journal). What do you want to accomplish, do or be? Who else is involved, if anyone? Where do you want to be? Picture the entire scenario and fill in all of the details. This is your success story and it should be as complete as possible.

Review your description and correct it, add to it, or change any part that suits you. When you feel that it is exactly as you'll want it, allow your body and mind to relax for a moment.

After becoming fully relaxed again bring back the picture of your success scene in full detail. Allow the scene to fill your mind as you remain relaxed. As you enjoy the feelings of success in your desired venture, notice what they are. Do you feel calm, empowered, joyful, excited, energized, or all of these?

Picture the scene for five or ten minutes, allowing yourself to revel in the good feelings that come from the experience of your success. When you feel ready, slowly open your eyes and continue to enjoy the feeling of personal strength that comes from experiencing success. Record your success scene on the page below or in your personal journal.

Your success scene:

_____

_____

_____

_____

_____

This experience will now be translated to your daily life as you fulfill your dreams and desires by acting on what you have pictured in your imagery practice. Be certain to tailor your self-talk to match. Whenever you find negative self-talk arising, you will have this powerful vision of success to counteract it, as well as the positive statements you have constructed.

Here are some of the experiences of people who have done this exercise:

"My negative scenes have one central theme even though one is work-oriented and the other relationship-oriented. The central theme is rejection with the comment 'I don't want you. You are not good enough.' This is my worst nightmare! When I saw my negative scene disappear into smoke, I felt a great release of pressure and anxiety.

"My negative scenes play out the nightmare of rejection while my personal positive image is set 20 years from now. I am with my loving spouse who tells me how our love and commitment have grown and enriched each other's lives. When I constructed my positive scene, I could feel myself becoming energized, and a smile crossed my face. My breathing became steady. I had a sense of knowing I could do it, be it, love it."

"Picturing the colors was difficult at first. I found that I couldn't get the colors to totally occupy all of the corners of my mind. I had resigned myself that this exercise would not work for me, so I went on to others. I thought these would be easier to accomplish. However, they didn't flow as easily as I had expected them to.

"I set the entire program aside and vowed to return to it later. It was during this period that I realized why the color exercise did not go well and why the others seemed to resist me. I had not allowed my mind to focus totally on the exercise. Just as the colors would begin to flow, I would let other issues invade my consciousness and I would focus my attention on them momentarily. This brief invasion made it difficult to paint my entire mind with the transition of the colors. I found it absolutely necessary to clear my mind prior to doing these exercises. As a matter of fact, after reviewing the color exercises again, I found that if I could not stop the bombardment of ideas or thoughts, it was best to set this aside, think about the interruptions, and then come back to the color exercise.

"I learned something else about the color exercise. If I completed it successfully, it was a great technique to relax my mind so I could complete the other exercises with more fulfillment. Although the exercises appear to be basic at first, they logically guided me from one step to the next. I personally feel that if I had eliminated one step, it would have been very difficult to reach the final conclusion."

Matching Self-Talk and Imagery

It is important to match your self-talk to your vision or image of success. We will practice writing self-talk statements that reflect what you really want from life.

Using as a model the list of positive statements that you previously made, construct a list that reflects your feelings about your success image. Write this list carefully, as you will want to return to it periodically to reinforce your new feelings about change and growth.

Examples:
    I am empowered by the strength of my vision.
    I am bursting with strength and vitality.
    I am intelligent and competent.
    I feel like a million dollars!
    I am excited and energized by my success.
    But of course! I'm just that wonderful!

Success list:

_____

_____

_____

_____

_____

_____

Powerful Life Experiences

Another area that deeply affects and shapes our lives is the **powerful positive and traumatic experiences** or events of our lives. Those of us over a certain age remember very clearly what we were doing the day that President Kennedy was assassinated. The power of that moment is recorded deep in our emotional memory banks. We *feel* the moment when we remember it. I was speaking to a young woman recently. She said that her emotional moment was the day the *Challenger* exploded. It is a day that she will remember all of her life and she will continue to be affected by it.

Dr. Morris Massey is a nationally known business consultant. He has analyzed the way in which our values are programmed into us. His conclusions are explained in a series of films which demonstrate the theory that *What We Are Is Where We Were When....*

His theory is that our values, prejudices and reactions to change are influenced by the era in which we were born. The events surrounding our lives as we grow up shape our worldview and belief systems. For example, people born before World War II have a strong belief in topdown management, hard work, long workdays and living within one's means. People born after World War II believe in participative management, time for creative development on the job, and credit buying. Life is never quite that simplistic, but it is useful for us to investigate whether what we believe is "natural" is only natural for the times.

Dr. Massey states that the most powerful effect of his work has been the response of people from different worlds who happen to be significant in each other's lives. A young man from Canada wrote him a letter saying, "I don't know who you are or what you do, but I want to thank you. I was a conscientious objector during the Vietnam war and I moved to Canada. My father had not spoken to me since. Dad saw your video at General Motors and called me to say that it was time we got together again. Thank you for giving me back my father." Dr. Massey says that the payoff for his work is people being moved at a personal level.

In all of our lives there have been powerful experiences, both positive, and negative or traumatic. Most of us have faced the loss of a loved one. We have had to deal with the pain and denial–and ultimate acceptance–of death. We have also perhaps faced other losses, like the loss of a job or the loss of a house. We may have been fired or demoted. We may have flunked a course in school or flunked out of school altogether. On the positive side, we have all experienced the birth of child, either our own or that of dear friends. We have found new jobs, gotten promoted, received awards. We have enjoyed the thrill of success. It is important to *feel how those events felt, deeply, subconsciously, at a nonrational gut level,* in order to understand some of the feelings that persist in our memory.

Even though we may not now consciously remember all the events, the way they felt stays with us. You may not recall how you got locked in the closet when you were two years old, but you may have a deep dread lurking in your subconscious mind as a result. These buried feelings may rear their heads and affect us in the present. The feelings are still there, even though the specifics have been lost.

In the same way, we have feelings attached to our positive experiences: receiving our graduation certificate; being praised by a co-worker; loving a special person. We can similarly draw on those

---

Many of us expect that joy is going to come from the environment, but we can't get joy from "out there."
*If you **experience** joy it is because you **express** joy.*

Bill Bahan, D.C., "The Heart of the Healer"

feelings of being loved and appreciated to condition our present reality. In this next exercise we recall those feelings. We will utilize them again and again as we build on our strengths.

Exercise
The Agony and the Ecstasy

The Agony: Moments of sadness and despair in my life:

Examples of Agonies:
    The loss of a loved one.
    Having a job change for the worse.
    Getting a divorce.
    Staying involved in a bad relationship.
    Leaving a place and people I love.

Your Agony List:

_____

_____

_____

_____

Examples of feelings:
    I felt depressed about my life; my future looked dim.
    I felt hurt and in terrible emotional pain.
    I felt that I was in the bottom of an abyss and that I would never get out.
    I just wanted to stay under the covers and sleep forever.
    I wanted to get into the car, roll up the windows, drive around town at three A.M. and scream.
    I wanted to punch somebody but everyone's bigger than I am.

How You Felt:

_____

_____

_____

The Ecstasy: Moments of happiness and joy.

Examples of moments of ecstasy:
    Receiving my diploma.
    Getting a new job I really wanted.
    Getting a divorce.
    Receiving an award for excellence.
    Being a member of a winning team.
    Being with people I love and who care for me.

Your Ecstasy List:

_____

_____

_____

_____

_____

Examples of feelings:
    I felt joyous.
    I felt empowered.
    I felt wonderful about my life and the people in it.
    I loved getting up in the morning and starting my day.
    Life felt terrific and exciting.

How You Felt:

_____

_____

_____

_____

_____

The memory of our agony and ecstasy and the feelings that accompany them will help us learn to access the feelings that empower rather than weaken us.

In order to profit by the experience of reliving our agonies and our ecstasies we can anchor, or strengthen, the feelings of ecstasy in our memory by associating them with a physical behavior. For example, if you reread your list of ecstasy moments and feelings and as you do, touch your hands together, you will strengthen the ideas in your mind.

Character

Character is composed of the set of inner characteristics we choose to express consistently. We all have all the character we need; the difference comes in the ways we choose to express it. It is easy to excuse our actions on the basis of the character we have built for ourselves:

"I could behave better, but if I do, people take advantage of me."

"I don't really feel good about this, but everyone else is going along, so I will too."

"I would succeed if only I were more (level-headed/ math-brained/ witty/ people-oriented)."

"I cannot rise to this challenge because I am not (assertive/ attractive/ strong) enough."

"I'm too vulnerable and sensitive for this kind of thing."

"I would like to make changes, but after all, I just work here. I'm not the boss."

"I wonder why I can't maintain relationships. Could it have anything to do with the way I treat people?"

We all have both positive and negative aspects to our personalities. We have both the capacity for love, gentleness and compassion and the capacity for anger, resentment and greed. As both sets of behaviors reside within us, we have a choice as to which we display in a given situation. Whichever set of characteristics we choose most often is strengthened and becomes predominant. So through what we choose to express, we determine our character.

We have many opportunities to nurture great character. We demonstrate it every time we choose to help rather than hurt someone. Each time we forgive another, each time we tell the truth, each time

---

Every time we choose to love rather than choosing to fear, we strengthen the habit of love. The sum total of our choices determines our character.

Dawson Church, "Communing With the Spirit of Your Unborn Child"

we accept responsibility for our decisions and our actions, we strengthen the habit of good character.

There are times when we rise to the occasion, when we accept the challenge and act without blame or excuses, when we express our integrity and honesty. Most of us have people in our lives whom we feel confident we can trust. We feel comfortable making a contract with them because we know that the contract will be honored. We know that we can confide in them because they will honor that confidence. We know that if they say they will do something it will be done. We know that if there is a need or a great cause, they will meet that challenge. We know these things because their actions have, consistently over time, expressed the values of their character.

Dr. Karl Jurak is a world renowned agrobiologist and biochemist. In 1922 he was granted his first Ph.D. for the development of a formula that increases physical energy. For 60 years he shared the formula with family and friends as a gift.

Dr. Jurak's inventions have always been in the service of others. In 1938 he developed water-based latex paint from plants. He worked on this project in response to a friend telling him that painters often died young due to lead poisoning from the paints they used. He is also the inventor of a freeze-drying process for vegetables that maintains their nutritional value and freshness without preservatives.

Although Dr. Jurak has nothing against money, his primary motivation has always been doing what he loves and in the service of others. He says, "If you do what you love, it may not pay at first, but it will eventually lead to monetary reward. I became a millionaire without even knowing how. The money just came in, I never knew where or how."

Dr. Jurak's strength of character is tied to Purpose in his work. His life has been dedicated to a career that he loves and to creations that enhance the quality of human life. He says, "No one in this life should do something they do not love. The real thrill comes from doing what you love! If you love your work, your work is your soul, your whole being."

We develop a picture of ourselves from a combination of our genetic heritage, our learning history, our self-talk, our life experiences and our

---

As long as you think of others first and yourself second, your success will come. This is certain.

Dr. Karl Jurak

strength of character. We continue to build on the best of all of these resources as we learn how to be true to ourselves.

Life Is Passion

Why is being true to yourself so important in understanding who you are? When we act in a way that is true to our nature, we create out of the core of ourselves the great, noble, fine center of our being. When we express the best that is in us, we enjoy an inner contentment that is unshakable. Our faith in ourselves is renewed daily. We open ourselves to be caring and free.

When we act without integrity in our work, or give anything less than all we have to give, then we have lost our greatest gift: ourselves. You cannot cheat another without cheating yourself. If you are waiting to be all that you can be, you are missing the opportunities you have to be great right now. But if you act from your deepest self, you will never be expressing less than you are.

The U.S. Army today uses a recruitment slogan that speaks to the potential in each person: "Be all that you can be!" This idea takes into consideration the fundamental drive we have to recognize and express our higher selves. *Personal fulfillment demands constant joining of behavior and actions with spirit.* If you do not live truth in each moment that you live, you do not create anything worthwhile. You cannot hold yourself back from risk and still live life fully. Life is passion.

Passion is single-minded dedication to the creation of perfection. The word "perfection" when used in this sense does not mean a static end goal in which everything is fixed and fine. It means a state in which we are pouring our fullest into everything that we do. When we live life with passion we refuse to allow obstacles to block us from living life fully.

In my Pathwalker workshops, perfection is an issue that surfaces frequently. In its own way perfection can be a block all its own. There are some people who use perfection (or the lack of it) as an excuse to procrastinate. "Well, when I get my ideas together precisely as they

---

Ultimately, man should not ask what the meaning of his life is, but rather he must recognize that it is he who is asked. In a word, each man is questioned by life; and he can only answer to life by answering for his own life; to life he can only respond by being responsible.

Dr. Viktor E. Frankl, "Man's Search for Meaning"

with this relationship and I'm sure I'm right, I'll communicate with my spouse." "When I really have had enough singing lessons and I have a voice like a songbird, I will sing for other people." Other people may even use the concept of perfection as an excuse to avoid something altogether. "I'd love to make my own furniture, but I could never possibly be good enough." "I'd love to go into the field of interior decorating, but I don't have a degree and it costs money to get started." "I'd love to have a relationship, but after all they take so much time and energy and you have to *relate!*"

Why do individuals choose to allow themselves to be blocked? We simply do not yet understand the price of the selfishness of our neuroses. *Each time we hold back we deny our strength and our faith in ourselves.* Every time we say "I'll *try* to grow" rather than just growing, we deny life. As Dr. Ken Blanchard says, "Trying is simply another way of not doing."

Who we are is the very best of what we do. Passion demands that we offer our best talents, our wholeness. When we act in good faith and give the best of ourselves to the world, we make a giant leap in faith. We move from a small space, filled with fear and anxiety, to a world of excitement, change and growth. This is the path of the heart. The path of the heart is expressed as we accept and use our talents and capabilities for the highest good of self and the blessing of others. We can be relaxed as we see life unfolding, knowing that we have demonstrated the integrity that is ours deep inside.

It is important for us to remember that there is nothing outside of us that makes us who we are. The determination of who we are is totally dependent on how we view ourselves.

Look inside to find your own perfect worth and the world will respond to that. Live your life always with Passion. Elizabeth Taylor called her perfume Passion because passion is an essential ingredient of her life. Make it an essential ingredient of yours.

On the next several pages are exercises designed to enable you to identify *who* you are and to help you discover your greater purpose in life. Once you have completed these exercises you will have a clearer sense of what is truly important to you, what brings you joy and peace, and what the direction of your life is meant to be.

The quality of a person's life is in direct proportion to their commitment to excellence, regardless of their chosen field of endeavor.

Vince Lombardi

Exercise
Personal Profile

Make a list of the following items:
1. My five most significant dreams and desires.
2. My five best skills and abilities.
3. My five best personal qualities.

My Five Most Significant Dreams and Desires:

1.

2.

3.

4.

5.

Example:
My five most significant dreams and desires:
- To be an accomplished motivational speaker.
- To have a beautiful home in the mountains.
- To live my life with integrity and passion.
- To live with caring and faith.
- To learn something new every day.

My Five Best Skills and Abilities:

1.

2.

3.

4.

5.

Example:
My five best skills and abilities:
- Writing
- Public speaking
- Motivating others
- Making people laugh
- Teaching

$$\boxed{\textit{My Five Best Personal Qualities:}}$$

1.

2.

3.

4.

5.

Example:
My five best personal qualities:
- Positive intent
- Honesty
- Intelligence
- Humor
- Integrity

Now, using all of this information about yourself, build a profile. A profile is a description of who you are right now. It is a description of the *real* you that you have begun to find through your personal research in life and in this book. It is the person you really like and want to know better.

As you make use of this information to create and reinforce a new you in your mind, you create a new reality. For example, I have always seen my Purpose as helping people to be all that they can be. I have been a counselor, a psychologist, a teacher, a manager and a consultant. Through each stage of my career my Passion has been to teach. The act of teaching itself has taken many different forms or Paths, but the Purpose has always been served.

Your profile will include the answers to the following questions:

1. I am...
2. I offer the world (gifts and talents)...
3. I am at my best when I am (doing)...
4. I enjoy life the most when...
5. I love...

Examples:

I am...a loving, caring, intelligent person.

I offer the world...my strength of character, my teaching ability, my integrity.

I am at my best when I am...teaching, writing, enjoying my friends. I am at my best when I am out in the desert camping, hiking and enjoying the sunrise. I am at my best when I am on horseback or playing golf. I am at my best when I am sharing lunch with a dear friend, talking and laughing. I am at my best when I am kind to people. I am at my best when I am helping someone.

I enjoy life most when...I am with people. When I am teaching. When I am out in the wilderness. When I am with my friends.

I love...life. I love my family. I love people. I love to teach. I love to talk to people. I love to write. I love adventure.

By answering these questions I have constructed a profile of a person who enjoys being with people, especially close friends and family; a person who enjoys communicating, counseling and teaching; a person who would most likely be at her best in an interesting environment, communicating in an easygoing manner. I have described the essence of my life.

My Personal Profile:

I am:

_____

_____

_____

_____

I offer the world (gifts and talents):

_____

_____

_____

_____

I am at my best when I am (doing):

_____

_____

_____

_____

I enjoy life most when:

_____

_____

_____

_____

I love:

_____

_____

_____

_____

Your Personal Profile has helped you to identify who you are now. It is a picture of the person that you really are, not the ego's picture shaped by fear, but the inner you shaped by growth. This picture is the essence of all that is courageous about you. It is all that is powerful about you. It is all that is fun, loving and thrilling about you!

Working from this picture strengthens and empowers you because it identifies the very best of you. Before we move to the identification of Purpose and Passion, let's use a marvelous tool that strengthens and imprints the work that we have just completed. This tool is called Affirmation.

Affirming the Best

An Affirmation is a statement formulated in the here and now that *connects what we want with who we are*. We say Affirmations every day without even realizing it. Have you ever said, "This is really a lousy day," or "Nothing is going right today," or "I will never get this job done on time"? If you have ever talked that way you have been affirming disaster. Why not affirm success?

Affirmations are our statements of positive self-value and intent. They are statements of our greatest desires for ourselves placed in the present time, which is the only real time there is. The past is past and the future has not happened. Our real lives happen *now*.

In order to work, Affirmations need to be positive, powerful and set in the present tense.

According to the *American Heritage Dictionary of the English Language*, "positive" means the opposite of "negative". I like that. It also means "admitting of no doubt; irrefutable." An Affirmation must be free of doubt in order to be effective.

"Powerful" means filled with energy, vigor and potency. We need to put all of our positive energy behind our Affirmations. They need to come from deep inside.

"Present" means in the here and now. When we put our desires into the future, they become wishes. This wish-filled future never arrives: it is the now that is real.

An effective Affirmation touches you at the gut level. You feel its impact when you say it to yourself. A good Affirmation is not a mere intellectual exercise; it is exciting, energizing, fantastic! This is why it is ultimately better to devise your own Affirmations rather than to accept one from someone else. It is your life that is calling!

It is a funny thing about life; if you refuse to accept anything but the best, you very often get it.

Somerset Maugham

Affirmations for Success:

- My life is filled with joy, love and prosperity.
- I am doing work that is interesting, enjoyable and lucrative.
- I am learning new things every day.
- My life is filled with the love of friends and with the companion of my dreams.
- I have a wonderful house on a lake and am able to travel whenever I want.
- I am in close contact with friends all over the world every week.
- I am healthy, wealthy and wise.

These may not be your Affirmations; they are simply examples of the types of Affirmations that people have successfully used in their lives. I have a short one that works when things seem to be getting out of hand and I find myself suddenly nervous. I simply say, "Everything will be just fine; it will turn out okay." It always does!

Find your own Affirmations by writing them down and trying them out. You will know which ones are right for you as you try them on: some of them will fit and some won't. The right ones are the ones that capture the essence of your growth. There are no generic Affirmations that work best for everyone. They need to be personal to you and your soul. You know what is right for you deep down. You know what your heart will listen to.

Your Success Affirmation:

I live in a wonderful place & am glad.
I am surrounded by friends who support me.
I have experienced wonderful things wth
Keep recurring.
I am able to do exactly as I want.

Pathwalker: Lucy Beale

Lucy Beale is an author and vice president of sales training for a telephone company. She is the mother of an 11 year old boy. Lucy is the creator and originator of the Win/Win Forum in Denver, Colorado. She is the co-author of *The Win/Win Way* (Harcourt Brace Jovanovich, 1987). and author of *Beyond Limits* (Sound Publishing, 1988).

The Authentic You

"I have known all my life that energy must be transformed from the lowest to the highest good and I have tried to consciously live this since I was 26 years old. I enjoy life immensely, creating unity through learning and teaching personal transformation through the Win/Win philosophy. I found how necessary this was through listening to my body.

"The contentment comes from helping others and allowing them to make changes in their lives; the Win/Win Forum has done that. Even seeming 'backslides' always turn out to be a step forward. Life is filled with wonderful things that have come from following my true path: health, abundance, a wonderful partnership, financial and psychic support to accomplish my mission, friends, travel and personal pleasures (such as material things). My joy is measured in moments, not things, and centers around my writing and speaking, my son, the mountains and my experiences there.

"Negative energy comes from my ego wants and desires, my reluctance to follow the path I have identified, societal programming and my own negative belief systems. But I am certain that these negative forces can be overcome by yoga, dreams, writing (especially 'journaling'), interactions with others, teaching, training, lectures, Affirmations, silence, mountains and desert, biking, skiing, hiking, herbs for balancing, knitting, sewing and sleep. In other words, when you are on the path of the heart, everything you do in life is part of that path and filled with excitement, change, and growth.

"I have always had vision. It simply is. Just as I have green eyes and I am five feet eight. Nothing can be done about it. It is my fact of life. It is to be taken for granted. Don't think about it; do it. Everything I do includes my vision. What is hard is to not live one's vision. That is ignoring oneself. Not living one's vision creates too much pain. It creates illness, bad relationships and lack of what you need for happiness. The result is aches, pains and complaints. Is that really worth it?

"Being true to yourself is essential, and we must do it. How do you do it? Turn off the TV. Turn off the stereo. Don't read anything but inspirational books. Go away alone. Stay alone. Find out who is in there. Learn serenity and silence. Your vision cannot be found by listening to the media or reading romance novels. Write in your journal daily. Keep your own counsel. Don't anesthetize yourself with drugs, alcohol, caffeine, cigarettes, chocolate and sugar. Be absolutely true to yourself. Do what is right for you. Never sell out your values, for then you sell yourself. Live your passion. Let work be play and vice versa. Don't believe what others say. Know what you know."

ADVENTURE

2

STEP

Finding Your Life's Mission

To be all that we can be requires giving up the trivial pursuit of survival and making the decision to live our Purpose and our Passion. It is so easy to be distracted by the desire to make money, to acquire material possessions and compete with those who possess all the symbols of accumulated wealth. Sometimes we choose a Path in life because it will make money rather than give us joy. Sometimes we choose a career because it will make someone else (parents, spouse or children) happy. Sometimes we just find ourselves on a Path and we don't even know how we got there; we are in a career that we just stumbled into. When we choose by not choosing, there can be no Passion.

Our Crystal Ball

Each of us has a crystal ball that we can consult in order to find the answers we need. This crystal ball is the small voice inside that tells us what is true for us. It is our inner knowledge of what our life is about. We always have the answers we are looking for inside us. They are the answers that come with extreme clarity and a gut-level sense of rightness. Unfortunately, these answers often come to us *after* we have done something that is less than worthy of ourselves, or made a decision out of fear or frustration rather than inner peace. Frequently, we do not listen to the inner voice of truth until we have already acted

> *There is no limit to the unfolding of oneself.*
>
> Tagore

and the tension is past. It is then that we must go back and fix or change what we have done.

We all have this inner knowledge. It is based in our past experience, our dreams, and our deepest basic truth. It is the accumulation of our life experience, our learning and our sense of justice. If we learn to use this built-in crystal ball, we can tap into our inner courage to live our Purpose and our Passion.

The crystal ball is always there. We are born with it. The information in the crystal ball is available to us to help us make appropriate decisions, to help us see our dreams and to affirm our desires. It does not require any magical ability to see into our crystal ball. It just takes practice.

Imagine your inner knowledge as a small multi-colored ball centered in the middle of your chest. Close your eyes and get quiet. Then choose an issue that has been worrying you. Frame it in the form of an important question; we will go to your waiting crystal ball for an answer. What question is important to you right now?

Your question:

_____

_____

_____

Exercise
The Crystal Ball

Go to a quiet, peaceful place where you will not be disturbed. Settle down comfortably and allow your entire body to relax. Clear your mind by picturing colors in your mind. Begin with the color blue. Allow the color blue to fill all of the spaces of your mind. Shift to the color green, the color of healing, and let it fill your mind. Allow the color green to fade slowly to the color yellow, the color of our sun. Enjoy the warmth

---

The time is at hand when men everywhere must forsake the fruitless search of the world at the circumference, and embark upon a courageous quest into inner space.

Eric Butterworth

---

of the color yellow filling your mind. Now shift to the color white as you release all tensions from your mind and body in preparation for your visualization.

Begin to look inside, to your center, in order to find your crystal ball.

As you look toward your center you will see a small round ball reflecting various layers of color. At the bottom of the ball is the color blue. Above that is the color green. Above that is the color yellow, and at the top is a brilliant, crystal-clear white. The top emits rays of bright light. As they emanate out from the crystal ball, they fill your body and mind with energy.

As you gaze into the blue level of your crystal ball, calmly remember your question. Ask for an answer and then relax and wait for an answer. Accept the answer in any form. It may come in the form of a feeling, a thought, a song, a picture or even a joke. Our answers come in many forms from our inner selves. It is important to accept the answer as it is presented. Don't insist on it looking a certain way. Accept whatever comes.

If you do not receive an answer in any identifiable form, move your attention to the next level, the green level. Ask your question again and then wait comfortably for an answer, knowing that one will come. If you do not feel that you have received an answer at this level, repeat the process after moving to the yellow level. Finally, if no answer is forthcoming, move to the white level. Often we need to get the answer a number of times before we realize that we have, in fact, received an answer.

The reason an answer may not be available until the white, yellow or green levels is that we may be deeply invested in an intellectual answer or in a fear-based response and we may be blocking our inner truth. It may require a little more inner focus and inner peace to enable us to hear the answer we truly need.

If you feel that you have not received an answer at any level, or that you do not understand the answer received, gently relax and let the process rest until a later time. Allow some time to pass, from a few hours to a week. You do not have to repeat the exercise continuously at one time.

If you truly have not received an answer at any level, continue to relax comfortably, open your eyes, record your question and arrange to do this exercise again. An answer will eventually come clearly to you.

If you have received your answer, open your eyes and record your answer in this book or in your personal journal. You may return to this information whenever you need it.

Your answer:

_____

_____

_____

Your crystal ball is there waiting for you whenever you are in need of an answer to your most pressing questions. It is a part of you; your creation, your own symbol. When we hear the voice of truth we also sense the power of our inner courage behind the voice. If we are willing to be still and go to our crystal ball in order to listen to our inner voice, we will make more and more Purposeful decisions.

Purpose is our reason for being. It is our overall sense of why we came here in the first place. It provides the greater picture of our life, the overview, the guide. Purpose moves us past survival, beyond fear and into the realm of faith in ourselves. Purpose gives our life meaning. It opens the way to Passion.

Passion is the demonstration of our Purpose in physical ways. Passion is demonstrated by the way we behave toward others, by the services we perform and by the attitudes we take. If we are living Passionately, then we are doing what we love and taking responsibility for that. If we are living Passionately, then we are joyful. Mother Teresa lives life Passionately. Harry Truman lived life with Passion as did his nemesis General Douglas MacArthur. Pavarotti lives life Passionately and so does Cher. We all have our dreams; the difference is that some choose to live them. We all take different Paths.

Our **Paths** are the directions in which we choose to take our Passion. Luciano Pavarotti, for example, might have chosen to run a pizza parlor and sing for customers. He could have shared his Passion with only a lucky few. He could have sung only in church, but he chose a career in opera and the world is grateful for that choice. Although

> *And the treasure of your infinite depths*
> *would be revealed to your eyes.*
>
> Kahlil Gibran

my Passion is teaching, it has taken different styles, different Paths. Writing, counseling, therapy, public speaking, corporate training–all are Paths to teaching. My message and my Purpose remain the same, to help people be all that they can be.

Focusing Our Inner Strength

Identifying Purpose, Passion and Path is the way to unlimited giving of ourselves with such focus and intensity that we burst at the seams with energy. We soar with uninhibited freedom. We refuse to be bound by known parameters and structures. We recreate all that is important to us in new and unimagined ways. This sense of having no barriers and boundaries is similar to the survival instinct that provides tremendous physical capabilities when we are under extreme stress. These powers are not apparent in times of calm or non-stress. Huge reserves of strength can work to keep us alive in conditions normally considered unsurvivable: severe cold, intense heat, deprivation. Lives are saved because of capabilities far and above those we are able to call forth in normal times.

When we are faced with life-or-death situations, a physiological mechanism called the primitive fight-or-flight response automatically takes over our bodily functions. When we are faced with severe physical danger (or *perceived* danger), our adrenal glands respond by pumping radically increased amounts of adrenaline into the bloodstream, increasing heart rate and blood pressure. Our breathing becomes quicker and more shallow. In response to these changes we have greater strength and stamina to either fight or run away. This mechanism helped our ancestors survive threats from their environment and is still with us today.

This is the mechanism that gave a 90-pound grandmother the strength to lift a 3,000-pound car that had rolled over her grandchild. When an Air Florida plane crashed into the Fourteenth Street Bridge in Washington, D.C., in 1982 there were many heroes. One young man, M. L. Skutnik, jumped into the freezing water to help a female victim to shore. She did not have the strength to reach the ropes thrown to help her. Mr. Skutnik threw off his coat and shoes and dove into the water to help her. Although he was exposed to freezing cold, he suffered no

Take your passion and make it happen.

From the movie "Flashdance."

ill effects. His attention was totally focused on saving the woman, and his body responded with the strength and protection needed for the job.

We all have this strength within us. We can call on it to help us do what we need to do and what we *want* to do. It is a matter of tapping into this strength and courage to assist our Purpose.

The journey of discovery draws forth the creative potential within us. When we open ourselves to the existence of our greater Purpose, we allow ourselves to become transformed, renewed and motivated. New energy comes from awareness.

When we want answers from within we must be still and listen. In the cacophony of daily life and the press of "things to do," we often miss important information. We all have a "little voice" that speaks to us and tells us the truth. You can tell the difference between your little voice of truth and the voice that nags you by the way you feel after you've heard it. If you feel at peace, empowered and fulfilled, it is the voice of truth. If you feel depressed or guilty, it is the nag. The nag comes from the outside in; the truth from the inside out.

The greatest gift that we can give ourselves is to be able to receive our inner gifts and to stay focused in our lives. The information that we need and the gifts that we require are always available to us. We simply need to gain access to them and be willing to work for ourselves and our growth.

The Magic of Focus

Why do we allow ourselves to be unfocused? Our survival needs are so great and our ability to meet those needs so spectacular—and yet they often remain untapped because of the lack of focus in our daily lives. Each of us must constantly remind ourselves of that source of power and energy that only awaits conscious attention to come forth in a burst of creativity and light.

Koichi Tohei is a master of Ki, or Chi, concentration. He is able to fight with five men at a time and—seemingly without touching them—lay them all out on the mat. He was a sickly child who studied the martial arts in order to develop his strength. Later he developed pleurisy and he turned inward to "reflect on the human condition." He found the human body to be weak and vulnerable and he felt that it

---

There are as many ways to live and grow as there are people. Our own ways are the only ways that should matter to us.

Evelyn Mandel

was our lack of focus in life that facilitated this weakness. He discovered the significance of concentrating one's inner direction on one point, the center of one's being. After a demonstration by one of his students in Hawaii, I was able to easily topple a man almost a foot taller and 70 pounds heavier than I was. Another time I was able to break a one-inch board in half with my hand. Having strength and focus is a great feeling!

French researchers Dr. H. Boon, Dr. Y. Davron and Dr. J. C. Macquet report that mind training of athletes improves their precision of movement, their economy of energy expenditure and their ability to control their balance and posture. Mind training, or training in focus, improves concentration and attention and enhances perception.

Dr. Barbara Brown, physiologist and biofeedback researcher, says in her book, *New Mind, New Body,* "With a slower heartbeat, mind efficiency takes a great leap forward." When we are focused, our heartbeat automatically slows down and we are better able to process incoming information. Being focused gives us the ability to learn better, make decisions better and live life more fully in the moment. We have more energy when we are focused because our energy and attention are not scattered.

The constant, unending, powerful stimuli that bombard us—telephones, news reports, family obligations, personal networks, tumbling thoughts and rush hour traffic—allow limited opportunities for achieving balance in our lives.

A sky diver friend of mine pointed out, "There's nothing like your chute not opening at 5,000 feet to focus your attention." Most of us rarely have the kind of jarring shock that an unopened parachute would provide. And so we drift. We do not live our Passion and demonstrate our true Purpose; we live second-hand lives, off-center, uncomfortable, vaguely incomplete. Living our Passion is a choice and we certainly are not forced to make it. In fact, we are free to ignore our Passion and Purpose and walk a comfortable, routine and familiar Path that offers no intensity, no perfection and no self-enhancement. We are free to live within our excuses and our "can'ts." Or—we are free to walk the Path less travelled.

Choosing Your Highest Purpose

How do you choose your Purpose and find your Passion? You find your Passion by making the decision to do so. We do not realize how many decisions we make about our lives every day. You may believe that "I am the way I am."

This is simply not true. We self-create every moment by making decisions regarding what we are capable of, what we "should" do and how we think other people view us. Instead of taking the time to ask ourselves what we really want to do, what would make us happy and fulfilled, we often move along an old Path without pausing to consider: it might just be a rut!

In determining what our highest Purpose is for being here, we must find what we love to do. When we commit ourselves to what we love to do, we demonstrate our willingness to give all that we are. True giving means total commitment. There are no valid halfway states. We are alive or we are not. We are committed–and act on the commitment–or we don't.

When our awareness of our Purpose is cloudy or dim and we see only fear and frustration, our vision is limited and our survival capabilities are reduced. When we see clearly and understand our Purpose, we see light-years and universes away.

A person who certainly lived his truth all of his life–but who did not live his true Purpose until after he was 65 years old–was Mahatma Gandhi.

For the majority of his productive years, Gandhi was a prominent and successful attorney in the finest British tradition. His personal values and integrity of action were always paramount. But his greatest moments lay within, waiting for the appropriate time in history.

It was after age 65 that Gandhi became the spiritual leader of the independence movement in India. In his speeches and actions, Gandhi articulated the laws of a greater truth, a truth that acknowledged the rights of human beings to live by their own direction and sovereignty.

Gandhi had a Passion: to help people, using the law. But he had a greater Purpose, which was to be the focus of the vision of his nation. His own essential strength of character, and his personal belief in moral and ethical right gave him the courage to put his ideals before the fear of death. Gandhi lived the power of truth.

We have Purpose in our lives to learn what we need to learn. It isn't always consciously altruistic, but it makes the world a better place to live. When we are acting out of the best of ourselves we are happy. When we are happy we give without thinking. Living our Purpose isn't heroic, but it requires courage. It isn't self-sacrificing, but it does require us to give ourselves over to an ideal. Purpose leads us into the valley of

---

Moral courage is not the exclusive province of extraordinary people—heroes and saints. It is available to anyone who lives his or her life routinely in relationships of care and concern for other people's welfare and for diverse groups of people.

Samuel and Pearl Oliner, "The Altruistic Personality"

the shadow of death: death of what we have clung to previously. It leads us into the release of limitations, release of old and harmful value systems, release of anxiety and fear, release of resentment and judgment against self and others.

Purpose requires concentration on that inner knowledge that resides in the place of the soul, and when we live in this place there is no room for fear or anger. Our greater Purpose, our reason for being here, guides us unerringly toward our best intent and our best behavior. Living our Purpose guides us into our life's longing to express itself through meaningful activity, our Passion.

The next meditation takes you on a journey back to your favorite place, the place that belongs solely to you. Your favorite place is a gateway to all that you will ever want or need. Each time you visit your favorite place you will find answers to your questions and peace for your heart.

Guided Meditation
Discovering Your Purpose

Find a quiet place where you will not be disturbed. Settle down in a comfortable chair, on the floor, or any place that will take your full body weight.

Begin to slow down your breathing and breathe deeply. Relax all of your muscles, head to toe. Relax your forehead, your facial muscles, neck, throat, shoulders, arms, upper back, lower back, chest, stomach, hips, legs and feet.

Check your breathing and your muscles. Is your breathing slow and deep? Are your muscles as relaxed as possible? As you relax that way, picture all of your worries as a black cloud. Allow that cloud to drift away from your head and out through the ceiling. See it dissipate in the atmosphere.

Once the black cloud is gone, fill your mind with the color blue. Let the color blue fill all the spaces of your mind, allowing you to relax even more.... Let the color blue fade and fill your mind with the color green. Green is a healing color and relaxes you even more deeply. Allow the color green to be replaced with a light bright yellow, like the color of the sun. Allow the color yellow to fill all the spaces of your mind. Finally, clear your mind using the color white. Now that your mind is clear you are ready for a wonderful journey.

Allow yourself to float away to your favorite place.... Fill in the picture with sights, sounds and feelings. What are the colors that stand out the most? Are there people or animals or entities of any kind? How do you feel? Are you joyful, peaceful, excited or wild? Is there a gentle wind, a bright sky, clouds or a soft rain? Get a clear picture of your favorite place with all the aspects that are important to you.

In your favorite place you will find the answer to the question, "What is my Purpose?" In your favorite place you will meet a messenger. The messenger may be a voice, a person, an animal, a flower or even an apparition. The message itself may be in the form of a letter, a song, a feeling, a gift-wrapped box or a simple suggestion. The message is the answer to your question, What is my Purpose?

The message may even be buried in some special place, in a treasure box or in an urn. Accept your message from the messenger. Read your message or hear your message; receive it in the appropriate way. Thank your messenger and then return the message to the place from which it came, for safekeeping. It will be here for you always and you can return for it whenever you choose.

If you did not receive a message, you may ask your messenger why. Sometimes the messenger will point out something that you did not originally notice. Sometimes the messenger will smile and in that moment you realize that you did receive a message and you know what it is. Sometimes the answer will appear in large white letters across the sky, lest you miss it.

If you did not receive a message the first time do not worry. The message is there and you will soon be able to receive it.

As you continue to enjoy the sense of physical and emotional relaxation, slowly stretch your muscles, open your eyes and reorient yourself to the room you are in.

Carefully, maintaining your meditative state, record in this book or in your personal journal what you have found.

My Greater Purpose:

Living Passion

Once you have identified your greater Purpose, the overriding reason for your life, it is time to identify your Passion. Your Passion is the expression of your Purpose in the work that you do. Many of us have spent too much time doing work that is unfulfilling because we have never taken the time to find out what we really want to do, what really brings us joy. When we are doing what we love to do, work is play. A friend of mine who has shifted from working for a department store to working at a job she really loves said, "I almost feel guilty getting paid for this. I'm having too much fun."

All limits aside, what gives you the greatest joy in your life? What do you enjoy doing the most? You have already got some clues from the Eagle Visualization and your Personal Profile. In the next exercise we will identify what drives you toward joy. We will zero in on the kind of work or service you would like to perform to fulfill your greater Purpose. What would make you want to jump out of bed each morning full of anticipation of your day? Passions may change their expression or form over time, but the basic Purpose remains the same.

Claire has moved from a career in management to a career as a professional singer through a process that, in retrospect, has a logical progression. Claire's transitions involved both risk and courage.

For ten years Claire was in advertising and marketing. By the time she left the field she was supervising forty people and was responsible for a two million dollar budget. She returned to college to get her M.B.A. and found the management environment both stimulating and attractive. Claire was aware that she was heading for a career change, and corporate training looked very satisfying. She discovered that "Training and education gave me an opportunity to be a 'ham.' I could have fun and still be in the business world. Helping people learn really motivated me."

Claire decided to work with a small company, which gave her an opportunity for more variety in her work. She continued to learn and grow in her new field and after a three-year apprenticeship she started her own company. As she puts it, "To me this transition seemed logical, but it was a high risk in terms of income and job security. I found that when I thought primarily of service to other people, I did well in terms of getting business. When I was in a state of fear, less work came."

During the eight years that Claire had her own consulting and training company, she began to go through spiritual changes and look inward. She questioned why she was present, living on planet Earth. She wondered what her greater Purpose was. She identified her Purpose as "Empowering myself and others, individuals and organizations, in the workplace and personal life." Underlying her

Purpose was the desire to give and receive love and to evolve as a person and as part of the human family.

Claire also wanted to discover her true Passion: "I wanted to have and use more creativity in my life. I began to write songs and discovered that this activity was a meditation for me. I write songs that help people love themselves and others."

The desire for more creativity led to Claire's next transition. In a stress class she took, one exercise required making a list of attributes or events that filled her with energy. One of her answers was music. So she bought a sing-along machine and created a structure to fill her with energy. She added singing to her corporate training, and began to sing at churches, weddings and other events. She found that her heart was pulling her away from corporate training, and she began to resist spending her time that way. She felt that she had already succeeded in that area, and she wanted a new challenge. As she listened to her heart, she felt the courage to begin the transition to the risky field of professional singing.

Claire is still in the process of building her new career. Although there is some anxiety in the transition, she has a clear-cut system for managing the change. The first thing she does each day is to relax physically, so that she doesn't feel hustled into the day. She has found that when she is relaxed, she is non-defensive, and easily able to express her personal energy.

The largest single block she faces in making her new career work is inertia. When you work for yourself as a singer, there are no deadlines. She faces the danger of just drifting along, allowing the drift to take her away from her greater Purpose. On the other hand, if she works too hard to overcome her inertia, she can lose sight of her Purpose amid stacks of things to do.

Another major block is the fact that, despite all the work, time, money and energy she is putting into singing, there are no visible accomplishments to be seen in the early stages. She has to remind herself of her greater Purpose and Passion on a regular basis. She observes, "When we are facing risk and change we often need to work at other jobs to support our change. It is important to find a job that you can enjoy or at least be peaceful in, even though it is not the thing you ultimately want. If we take work to support our goal, we cannot blame this work, because it is assisting us in reaching our goal. To help us remember this, we can ritually commit to our Passion and agree to give something to that Passion each day. The trick is to not become a victim. Each time you meet someone, introduce yourself as your Passion. I say, 'I am Claire, a singer.'

"Ask other people for help. Don't just pray. Ask your friends and acquaintances. People will be very helpful and give you all kinds of suggestions." Like the the old story of the preacher who was faced with death by drowning as the the river near his church began to rise. He prayed fervently to God to help him. Soon, rescuers came by in a jeep to pick him up. He refused their assistance, saying that he had faith that God would help him.

As the river continued to rise, the preacher was forced up to the roof to escape the foaming waters. He again prayed to be saved. Some people passing by in a boat offered to take him, but he refused their help, saying that he believed that God would rescue him. After a few hours the river had risen so high that the preacher was forced to take refuge by climbing to the top of the church steeple. He prayed to God to save him. A helicopter appeared and lowered a rope, but he refused, saying that his faith remained steady that God would deliver him.

The waters continued to rise, and the preacher was swept away by the river and drowned. As he faced God in heaven he asked, "Why–after such fervent prayer–did you not save me?"

God answered, "I sent you a jeep, a boat and a helicopter. What more did you want?"

If you want to make your life work, take responsibility. Claire has consistently taken responsibility for her own life and her own decisions. You can't do better than that!

In the Eagle Visualization you identified what you would love to do in your life. What was it? What did you want to do? Did you want to be like Hank Aaron, Lee Iacocca, Walt Disney, Margaret Mead, Margaret Thatcher or Indiana Jones? Did you want to be just like yourself, only more creative? What did your Personal Profile indicate to you? Let's pull out the essence of that information.

Summarize in this one place all of the information that seems most pertinent to you.

My Peak Experiences tell me that I feel most powerful when...

---

*It does not matter what we expect from life,
but rather what life expects from us.*

Viktor Frankl

My Eagle Visualization tells me that I have the most fun when...

My most important dreams and desires are...

My best skills and abilities are...

My best personal qualities are...

My Purpose in life is...

With all of this information in mind, let's prepare to return to meditation. This time we will ask our inner self about our most desired work, our Passion.

Guided Visualization
Finding My Passion

Find a quiet place. Get as relaxed as possible by relaxing your muscles and clearing your mind. Fill the spaces of your mind with the color blue.

Allow the relaxation to continue. Change the color in your mind to the healing color green. Notice the sense of total body relaxation as this cool color fills your mind.

Let the color green fade into the bright color yellow. Let the color yellow fade as you return to your favorite place. While in your favorite place you will meet a messenger. It may be the same messenger as before or a new one. This messenger will tell you about your Passion. The message may come in the form of an oral message, a note, a picture, a feeling, or even a body sensation.

After you receive your message, give it back to the messenger for safekeeping. It will always be there for you. Continue to relax as you open your eyes and record your message. Record your message in your personal journal or below.

Experiences

Your messenger may take many forms. The experience is different for each person. After this exercise, one man reported: "I had the image of a friend of mine who came as my messenger. She told me that I am a leader in this world, charged with the responsibility of sharing my knowledge to motivate other people. I have a destiny to bring messages of power and inspiration to many others."

Another participant saw her messenger in a different form: "I experienced my guide in the form of Jesus Christ. He took my hand. We stood before serene people and began to teach."

Yes, But...

What if you have a short attention span and constantly get distracted from your sense of Purpose? Sometimes we focus on Purpose for a while and then fall back into old patterns of thinking and feeling. Sometimes, even with the very best of intentions, we sabotage ourselves and go back to old habits.

When we discover the things that block us from achieving a strong sense of Purpose, we can then acquire tools to enable us to transcend them and move forward in our lives. When we become fully aware of our Path, we can no longer conform to the edicts and aspirations of the world outside us, and we become transformed through our belief in ourselves.

The affirmations that we have been practicing help to focus us on the positive aspects of our belief systems. Sometimes we need to *just stop thinking* as we did with our self-talk and immediately change to a positive statement. "Yes, but's..." are a great cue to us to do this. For example, when you catch yourself in a yes-but statement like "I'd really like to do that but...I don't have the energy/I don't have the money/I'm too old," STOP yourself at the word "but" and use that as a *cue word* to make a positive affirmation, like "I really want to do that and I am totally competent to do so." Some examples of "Yes, but's..." are as follows:

"You might want to go to night school for the training you need for the career you want."
"**Yes**, I could, **but** I don't really have the time/money/opportunity.

STOP: "That is a good idea. I am checking with my local college/ adult school/professional school right now!"

"In order to improve your relationship you may want to sit down and talk with your partner."
"**Yes**, that's a good idea, **but** I'm not really good at that/my partner doesn't understand me/my partner understands me all to well and I don't like it!"

STOP: "Yes, I am calling my partner right now to arrange to talk through the voice of love.

"I really need to get on an exercise program."
"**Yes, but** I am so very busy that I just can't find the time."

STOP: "I am making the time."

Whenever we hear our minds saying statements like the ones above, or our mouths about to say them, we are served a reminder to become positive in our thoughts and statements. Each step in the process is equally important.

- **Step One:** Catch the cue of each "Yes, but" statement in your mind, preferably before it reaches your mouth.
- **Step Two:** Yell STOP in your mind and picture a large red stop sign.
- **Step Three:** Replace the negative statement immediately with a positive one.

There is an alternative that we have not yet discussed. If you realize, after making the positive statement, that you know you won't be able to follow through with it, then reconsider the whole situation. For example, if you realize that you are not going to communicate with your partner, you may need to reconsider the relationship as a whole. You are not committed without communication, so accept this as a message that the situation needs work.

If you know, after you have made a positive statement about exercise, that you are not going to do it, release the need to exercise. If exercise is something that you feel you should do rather than something you can learn to love to do, just let it go. If you want to lose weight but you are unsuccessful at "dieting," rethink your strategy. There are studies that indicate that people who go on and off many diets are less healthy than those who either diet and maintain their weight, or who choose not to diet at all.

Living your life appropriately means committing to a continuing series of thoughtful decisions. Your life is, in fact, as valuable as you make it, and simply being conscious of the "yes, but's" that go on in your mind will make an enormous difference in the quality of your inner dialogue.

All these things shall love do unto you that you may know the secrets of your heart and in that knowledge become a fragment of Life's heart.

Kahlil Gibran

Bonding with Purpose and Passion

Identifying and acknowledging our Purpose takes us into a truly different plane of existence. By acknowledging our dream and turning it to action, we create a new reality for ourselves and those around us. Living our Passion is an act of love.

Finding our Purpose is easy since we are bonded to it and by it. To begin to discover our Purpose, we must be quiet and receptive, away from the stimuli of daily life. We must be open to messages from our inner selves. As we receive and accept our Purpose and its demonstration, our Passion, we become empowered; we believe anew. No longer must we conform to the demands of the outside world or of other people. We are now fully aware of the spirit within and capable of starting the process of creation in our daily life.

Our Purpose and Passion pull at us. Even if we try to live lives of unconsciousness, they demand recognition at the back of our minds. We always have the choice to answer the call and soar with the eagles, or feel the pain of self-rejection. We recognize that feeling; it is the pain of boredom, malaise, unaccountable irritability, anger or depression. This pain and frustration can serve a useful purpose: it can motivate us to open to our greater Purpose. Pain does get our attention, after all; by showing us where we are stuck, pain opens us to growth!

Consistently focusing on your Purpose moves you into a place where a reservoir of talent, ability, creativity, energy, courage and resilience reside. As you tap into this resource, you attune yourself to the knowledge and energy of the universe. You access the collective unconscious of all time and you begin to connect with the truth of your inner being, the self that knows what your reality and Purpose are.

Life Is Growth

The essence of all life is growth. Living things either grow or die. The essence of all growth is change: you cannot grow and not change. The growth of a person often involves risk. For human beings change can seem undesirable, scary, even threatening. We tend to be more comfortable with the familiar, even if we are unhappy, bored or

---

The unexamined belief system is not worth having.
The unexamined life is not worth living.

William Wordsworth

frustrated. Getting people to change their lives without their own commitment to do so is almost impossible.

Our sense of Purpose is what moves us from just thinking about change from a position of inertia to actually doing something. A sense of Purpose is the motivating force that keeps us going. Humans need a cognitive awareness of their Purpose in order to live it. The danger lies in ignoring the message and going off in inappropriate and unhappy directions.

Nature receives its direction from within and follows its own divine plan. A good example of this is the seed. There is a genetic imprint in the seed that guides it to extract energy from the soil and the sun. The seed grows and fulfills its genetic destiny, not because it has a conscious awareness of its Purpose, but because it has the power of focus within its structure.

This is demonstrated by the growth that occurs. The seed draws substance from the earth around it to sprout and send out roots to attract the nutrients in the soil needed for survival. The seed sends up shoots to gather precious sunlight that will enhance and continue the growth. There isn't any outside source to teach the seed what it must do. Its genetic imprint allows the natural course of life to occur. In time, the seed has leaves and flowers that become part of an interdependent cycle in nature that brings its Purpose to fulfillment as the mature fruit of the seed interacts with other life forms. All of this is programmed into that tiny bit of matter.

What I've just described is the easy way. This example assumes the seed is living in lush, fertile and welcoming soil. But what if the seed falls into a crevice? What about the seed lying on rock, in sand, in a desert? The small and vulnerable seed will find a few ounces of soil and against all odds will actualize itself by the sheer power of its genetic Purpose. It will tenaciously take hold, perform its programmed functions, expand, grow and live. The seed can grow in the most unwelcoming areas of the rock. And not only that: once it has taken hold, it may eventually break even the bonds of the rock, splitting the rock and making room for more life. The seed asks no questions about why it is here and what it is for. It is imprinted with its answers.

We are also imprinted with our answers, but being sentient beings, we need to ask the questions. If we do not ask the right questions about our Purpose and how it is revealed through our Passion; if we instead choose to ignore our Purpose in order to seek security, money, fame or simply survival, we succeed in covering up that spark of intelligent, Purposeful life that forms our essence. Unlike the seed, we have the power to deny and thwart our growth. *Finding the Great Creative You* is all about uncovering that inner spark of Purpose and fanning it into the flame of Passion.

Another example is the caterpillar, which although it has no awareness of its ultimate destiny, has the potential of being a butterfly coded within its genetic structure. This potential will be activated when the the creature is ready. When this activation occurs, when the chrysalis is entered, there is a radical transformation. As it grows, it becomes something new.

Just like the butterfly, Purpose has a plan to activate the metamorphosis process and help us align with our greater good, our true Path. Unlike the caterpillar who must fulfill its physical destiny, we human beings can block our spiritual destiny by refusing metamorphoses. Temptations assault us constantly to be less than our greater good.

The positive side is that as humans, our sense of Purpose becomes greater as we grow beyond the mere instinct that drives the caterpillar and the seed. As we expand into higher realms of understanding, our need for growth moves us past the drive for survival. We move to our unique human quest for knowing. We feel strong urges to fulfill our desire to give, create and make the world a better place to live. Throughout our lives, growth occurs through new knowledge, encounters, experiences and relationships. These are the chapters of our lives, the demonstration of who we are. They tell the story of our opportunity to manifest our best to the world.

Like the seed growing in rock or desert, we can succeed against all odds, since the only limitations we place on ourselves are our belief systems. If we change our thoughts, we change our lives. Challenging our perceptions and assumptions helps us to change our thoughts. Negative beliefs are one of the major challenges that we face when changing our lives.

Tom Sullivan is a successful actor, a professional musician, an amateur athlete and a best-selling author. Tom Sullivan is also blind. He had the choice of several paths in his life. One would have led him into despair and bitterness–and the other to self-esteem and success. Like the seed that fell onto stony ground, Tom had his challenges in life, but he also had his strengths.

Tom fought much of his life to be accepted in the sighted world as an equal. His true success came after he learned to accept his blindness and use it as a positive force. Through his life experiences and choices he learned that he was special in the most positive sense. He made the most of his special talents, his special personality and his inner self.

He turned his frustration and his supposed handicap into a series of successes. He rowed in the 1967 Henley Regatta and tried out for the 1968 U.S. Olympic wrestling team. He began to arrange music, and wound up working with some of the biggest stars in the business. He plays golf and basketball, swims, jogs and sky-dives. Tom enables himself to do what he himself chooses to do, rather than what he has been told that blind people can do.

There was a time when Tom was a selfish and self-centered person. He had very high expectations of others, of what he felt they owned him because of his disability. He was most demanding of those who loved him. He was full of anger, self-pity and misunderstanding of himself and others. He often tried too hard and was overly competitive. In the earlier part of his life, winning was everything and people were secondary.

Tom overcame a number of stumbling blocks in order to clear up his life and see himself as a treasure and a gift. He overcame fear, failure and envy. He learned to accept the word "no" when appropriate. He taught himself to deal with the negative self-comparisons he had been making with others, with his excessive competitive drive, with his anger. He says that "Each person is in control of his life. Each person must evaluate himself, his wants, needs and talents. No one can do it for him."

In his book entitled *You Are Special*, Tom observes: "I believe there are moments in our lives that shape, dominate, and control our destiny. Within each, we hold options–options that make it possible for us either to move forward and upward in the spiral of mental, physical and emotional evolution or to fall back into pits of depression, despair and dependence. I don't think any of us can honestly look at our lives without being able to recognize our own particular turning points. I think we can look to these turning points as clear-cut barometers for answering the question, 'Did we move toward positive life-involvement when confronting these choices?' "

Tom had a belief system that allowed him to overcome the challenges that life presented him and to excel even when a sighted person might not. He could have gone in a number of different directions in his life, yet he chose metamorphosis and growth. He chose the Path of fulfillment. Each of us has the same opportunity in life to choose the Path that we will take. Each of us has our own "handicaps" to overcome, our own stumbling blocks. Our personal handicaps are our negative belief systems, our refusal to take responsibility for our lives and our fear. Our strength comes from choosing the fullness of life over our excuses and our can'ts.

To stumble is not to fall.

Tom Sullivan

Negative Belief Systems

We sometimes have a belief system that says that our thoughts are not within the realm of our control, that they are events that happen independently of us. That particular belief system is the major block to self-fulfillment. As long as we believe that we are the "victims" of our thoughts we are vulnerable to self-deceit.

The fact of the matter is that *we are always in control of our thoughts*. We are the creators of our thoughts, not the victims. Negative beliefs can be our greatest blocks to success. If our thoughts were not under our control, then we could never change our minds. We could never change our viewpoint and we could never change our perceptions. When we accept responsibility for our thoughts and beliefs we are on the right track, the growth track.

Dr. Viktor E. Frankl is the creator of *logotherapy*, a form of therapy that focuses on the future and defuses the negative thinking and feedback mechanisms that create neurosis.

Dr. Frankl was a prisoner in Auschwitz during World War II. In this extreme situation, he discovered that people always have control of their inner atmosphere of attitudes and feelings. In his book, *Man's Search for Meaning*, Dr. Frankl relates his experience of the possibility of both human kindness and human cruelty in extreme situations. Of his daily routine in the death camp, he writes:

"And there were always choices to make. Every day, every hour, offered the opportunity to make a decision, a decision which determined whether one would or would not submit to those powers which threatened to rob you of your very self, your inner freedom; which determined whether or not you would become the plaything of circumstance, renouncing freedom and dignity to become molded into the form of the typical inmate.... Fundamentally...any man can, even under such circumstances, decide what shall become of him–mentally and spiritually. He can retain his human dignity even in a concentration camp."

This discovery, that our inner processes are under our control no matter how ghastly the outer circumstances may become, is one of the most important things we could ever learn. Frankl, Solzhenitsyn, and other writers have noted that it was the camp survivors who took

---

*He who has a why to live
can bear with almost any how.*

Friedrich Nietzsche

responsibility for maintaining control of their inner climate who tended to survive, despite receiving the same terrible treatment as all the others. Those whose inner worlds were conquered by the brutality of the outer world were more likely to succumb.

The reality that we all have control of our own thoughts is a powerful tool for changing ourselves and our world. In the chapters to come, we will put it to use in creating the kinds of circumstances in our lives that we know are possible.

Fear may paralyze, but dissatisfaction can be the greatest motivator to change. The United States would never have been founded if the early settlers had been satisfied with the degree of freedom they were given as a colony. It would never have been discovered at all if Columbus had been satisfied with the existing sea-land route to India! Dissatisfaction with our lives can serve to drive us to higher goals and greater fulfillment opportunities. And yet, depending upon how it's viewed, dissatisfaction can also cripple and blind us if we become mired in a sense of helplessness, depression and powerlessness.

Growth always offers a certain amount of discomfort. If we resist it, we human beings have the remarkable power to block our own metamorphosis, never knowing the fulfillment of achievement. Or, by moving with the Purpose and Passion brought to us by life's process, we can acknowledge our potential and free ourselves to blossom into our full destiny. The focus of our life then moves from survival and physical stability to awareness of the soul's growth and unfolding. As we commune with the universal process of unfolding life, all experience becomes our bread, all learning becomes our wine. Our souls are sustained as we blossom.

Moving from Victim to Victor

Purpose takes us into an entirely different plane of existence. We get less caught up in the limited thinking of "making ends meet," and instead take a dream and turn it into action. We create a new reality for ourselves and find a way to offer that reality to others.

Consider Terry Fox. Terry found Purpose and translated it into millions of dollars for cancer research that would ultimately benefit many other people. After a bout with cancer that left him with only one leg, he decided to make a statement. He strapped on an artificial

The only thing we have to fear is fear itself.

Franklin Delano Roosevelt

leg and ran thousands of miles across Canada to capture world attention about the need for cancer research.

Terry could have sat back and said, "What can I do? How can a person with one leg accomplish something in life?" If Terry had said, "All my dreams and hopes are ruined. I can never accomplish the things in life that I wanted to," he would have truly been crippled and Purposeless. In the beginning, Terry had little but determination, a sense of his own Purpose and the support of his family. But on he ran, cold, lonely and often in great pain. Slowly his Purpose, his dream, caught on and took hold in the minds of others. Others shared his excitement as he fulfilled his soul's need to demonstrate Purpose and make the world a better place to live.

Terry died, but with the recognition by others that he had lived completely, that he had been actualized in a powerful way. Like Terry, we have a choice.

Why should we bother to live our Purpose, especially if it causes pain, hardship, or difficulty? Because, ultimately, if we drift through life perfecting the art of making excuses and wallowing in reluctance and doubt of our abilities, we create a narrow, insignificant, meaningless Path. If we make these choices, our death will leave no ripple on the surface of the earth we walked. This is a monumental, scary freedom. We all have the power to ignore our Passion, live outside of ourselves, live an unexamined life and believe that we are not unique.

To live your Purpose brings you joy. This sense of fulfillment is like no other experience. Living your Purpose allows you to experience the energy created by striving toward the heights of which you are capable. You are in control of your life and you are powerful! Write this down three times below:

I am in control of my life and I am powerful!

> *If you aren't part of the solution,*
> *you're part of the problem.*
>
> Eldridge Cleaver

Living in Control

The essence of life is right now. Every moment we live life anew; there is no past and there is no future. A friend of mine in Japan taught me an essential lesson of life. I happened to be complaining about the lack of a suitable view from the balcony of my apartment. My apartment overlooked a lumberyard and a dump.

My friend taught me to look at, rather than the whole scene, the one square inch that holds the beauty of life. He taught me to see the one perfect flower growing by the side of the road. He taught me to see the clear patch of blue sky above me. He taught me to see the phone booth down the street with the bright red telephone inside. He taught me to see the joy in the eyes of the children passing by. He taught me to see the small perfect pictures of life that we pass by and miss every day.

When we are busy seeing the larger picture we may lose the square inches of life that remind us of life's continuity and why we are here. When we take control of where we turn our gaze, we can begin to focus on the solutions of life rather than the problems. Both are there, and we have the choice. We can choose to live life and break out of our bounds like the seed. If we pretend that our decisions, the responsibility for who we are and the quality of our lives are all outside of ourselves, we relinquish mastery over our destiny. There is no responsibility outside of ourselves. *We are in control.*

The Power of Focus

Focus puts power behind our Purpose. Focus comes from knowing what our Purpose is. When we are clearly oriented to what is important in our lives, we enjoy the power of focus. Whenever your mind is focused, it is as though you have brought your internal camera into visual clarity. Just as you focus the lens on a camera to clearly define exactly

I believe we are here to do good. It is the responsibility of every human being to aspire to do something worthwhile, to make a better place than the one he found. Life is a gift and if we agree to accept it we must contribute in return. When we fail to contribute, we fail to adequately answer why we are here.

Armand Hammer

what you want in the picture, personal focus enables you to hold an image of exactly what you want in your life.

The power of focused energy is exemplified by the laser beam. The laser beam is composed of light waves moving in step, in "spatial coherence." Waves of coherent light move together, in formation, and this coherent quality increases their power thousands of times. Laser light is highly concentrated and directional. It travels in a very narrow beam and the sides of the beam remain almost parallel. By contrast, the light from the sun, electric light bulbs, fluorescent lamps and other non-laser light sources travel out in all directions. Laser light also differs from other light in terms of frequency, or the number of vibrations per second.

The laser is so powerful because it is focused, directed and in phase. When exactly the same amount of energy is diffused or scattered, it has much less impact.

Our power, like the light rays, exists whether we focus it or not. If we choose to never bring our light to bear in a coherent way, it diffuses meaninglessly off into the cosmos. But when we focus the light of our Purpose through our Passion, we have the power of the laser beam. When we are focused, we are directed in our thinking, straightforward in our communication and we have abundant energy. Think about the times when you knew exactly what you wanted, when you were clear, and you moved steadily forward. Even the least assertive of us are empowered when we are focused.

When we are not focused, when we are diffused like the electric light, it is easier for us to be pushed off target. It is our Purpose that draws us to clarity of thought and directs us toward right action and good intent. Purpose grants us the ability to separate the meaningful from the extraneous in life. Like the seed, we can draw the nutrients we need from life. When we are living our Purpose, we give back the greatest of our energies and talents. With Purpose we can focus an embodiment of power far greater than we ever imagined.

Purpose is also like a magnet that attracts to it, from an abundant universe, all that it needs to unfold. We are no longer alone and helpless. Purpose draws to us support from others: when we are committed to our Purpose, people connect with that integrity of action and choose to support us. Focus allows the total honesty of who we are to be expressed through our behavior, our words and our feelings.

The following exercise will help to demonstrate the power of your own internal focus.

Exercise
The Power of Focus

To test the power of focus you will need a partner.

- Stand in the middle of the room.
- Lift your arm and point your hand toward a wall.
- Concentrate on the tips of your fingers as your friend tries to pull your arm down. He or she will probably have no problem.
- This time, lift your arm and point toward the wall. Focus your attention on your energy. Picture the energy of your body extending up through your arm and out to the wall. Then picture that energy passing through the wall and right out into the universe.
- Ask your friend to try to pull your arm down now. Most likely he or she will not be able to pull your arm down very easily.
- You will have increased your energy several fold through focus.

What you have demonstrated is the power of focus. When our energy is focused we have the energy of the laser beam. We have taken what is basic to us all and concentrated it in one direction. This is the gift of a focused life. When you are clear about what you want, all of your energy is concentrated in that direction. When you are focused and determined, you cannot fail.

Affirmations
Focus

This exercise will enable you to formulate your own focus affirmation for those times when you feel your energy is diffused. When you are feeling weak and out of focus it is important to stop what you are doing, find a quiet place and affirm your inner peace and power. An affirmation, to be useful, must be clear, precise, positive and written in the here and now. In order to regain focus when you feel diffused, it is important to first discover when you are diffused and then to release that feeling and refocus. Typically, you will find that certain recurring situations, called **trigger situations**, are the most likely to result in your being diffused. In these situations, simply noticing that you are

When asked by a stranger how to get to Mount Olympus, Socrates answered, "Make every step you take go in that direction."

diffused triggers the power of focus. The first step toward focus is identifying these situations.

You then have the opportunity to **release** the situation and your own diffused reaction. This second step of releasing gives you perspective. You then can introduce what you truly want into the situation, rather than being ruled by your old habits and reactions. Once you have distanced yourself by releasing, you can focus your energies in order to bring your full creativity and imagination to bear. The **focus affirmation** is a concise statement of your focused intention in that situation.

The following examples exemplify the three steps of identifying the trigger situations, releasing and re-focusing.

Trigger Situation:

I get diffused when I am overworked.

I get diffused when I am very tired.

I get diffused when I am under time pressure.

I get diffused when someone is angry at me or vice versa.

I get diffused when I am unhappy.

Release:

I am able to release the initial tension when I breathe deeply.

I am able to release the initial tension when I take a moment to stop and be alone.

I am able to release when I stretch and move my body.

As I breathe deeply I release all negative tension around this negative affirmation and prepare to replace it.

Focus Affirmation:

I am powerful in my Purpose and my Passion.

I am relaxed and in control.

I am focused and strong.

I am powerful in my being.

I live in full confidence of my ability to live my Passion and my Purpose.

I wake up each day filled with excitement and joy.

Bearing these examples in mind, write down some of the typical situations which trigger a feeling of powerlessness or being unfocused in you.

1. Trigger situation:

_____

_____

_____

_____

_____

2. Release:

_____

_____

_____

_____

3 Focus Affirmation:

_____

_____

_____

This exercise is designed to enable you to formulate your own focus affirmation for those times when your energy is diffused. When we are feeling out of focus it is important to stop what we are doing, find a quiet place and affirm our inner peace and power.

This is not meant to be a one-time exercise. In order to change old habits we need to give new habits our consistent attention. The first step, just as in negative self-talk, is to become conscious of when we are diffused.

1. You might **look for signs** like:

Feeling sleepy
Not paying attention
Being hyperactive
Being unable to sleep
Feeling anxious
Feeling irritable
Getting sick a lot
Feeling depressed

2. Once you notice one or more of these signs that you are diffused, begin to **notice your self-talk.** Are you saying things like:

I'll never get this done!
I can't stand this pressure!
Leave me alone!
I'm sick of this.
I'm so tired I can't stand it.
I just want to get away.
I just want to sleep.
I've got to change my life!

3. As soon as you identify that you are in a stress situation (diffused), immediately use your **release,** both verbal and physical. Say:

I am calm and serene.
I am breathing deeply, slowly and comfortably.

4. Move directly into **re-focus:**

I am powerful.
I am relaxed.
I am in control of my emotions.

If you have allowed your behavior to override these messages from your brain and you find yourself helplessly drifting further away, go to the work that you have done in this book, the work in your personal journal. Go to caring friends and get help. What you will receive from your writings is a graphic reminder of your strengths and resources, your successes and your great courage. From your friends, you will receive the help that you ask for.

Refining Affirmations

An acquaintance who is a corporate trainer uses Affirmations to help him to maintain sobriety and a positive self-image. He uses them in his professional life and says, "Before I do a class, I see myself getting the praise and appreciation of the participants. I affirm a positive outcome for the class and myself. I also use Affirmations for healthy relationships, something I never felt I was worthy of. I also call on them when I feel my shame process kicking in: I tell myself that this negative programming is a lie, God doesn't make junk."

Beverly Allen is a person who knows how to use positive Affirmations in her life to not only make things work, but to overcome disability. Stricken with multiple sclerosis, she was unable to walk or stand for longer than fifteen or twenty minutes at a time without great fatigue. Her vision became so bad that her visual field included only blurry shadows. She had trouble balancing her body when she walked and her speech was slurred. People often thought that she was drunk. "That was really their problem," she says. "I knew the truth and that was all that was important."

With all of the pain, discomfort and fatigue she still faced a house to take care of, two growing children, two dogs, and a husband whose job kept him away for weeks at a time. When asked how she managed to keep functioning with little energy, little help and very little strength, she said, "It had to be done, so I just went ahead and did it.

"I just kept believing. I practiced creative visualization and positive Affirmations for my healing. I was able to look inside and find my inner strength. I love my life and I fight for it. I make it clear to myself that I have a disease; the disease doesn't have me!"

As Bev Allen told this story in church, she stood strongly, walked easily and saw all of us clearly. Her M.S. is under control, she is growing stronger every day and she lives her life fully and completely. She has an attitude of strength and a belief in her personal ability to affect her own life positively.

Now is the time to write a crystal clear Affirmation and to refine it till it is exactly what you need. Take the time to refine it down to its

---

The salvation of man is through love and in love.

Viktor Frankl

essence. Make it so condensed and so potent that it empowers you every time you think it.

Read back over your list of Focus Affirmations and choose the one that appeals to you most at gut level, the one that really hits home. Close your eyes and breathe deeply. Think about the Affirmation that you have chosen. See if it feels meaningful and powerful to you. Open your eyes and rewrite your Affirmation three times until it sounds just right to you. Condense it until it is a pristine statement of your intent.

Example:

1. I feel good about myself and my ability to do what I need to do to live my Passion and my Purpose.

2. I am confident of my ability to live my Passion and my Purpose.

3. **I confidently live my Purpose and Passion.**

Your Refined Affirmation:

I am relaxed & in central
I can improve.

Practice does, in fact, make perfect. It is critical that you practice positive thinking and Affirmations on a regular basis. The brain, like nature, abhors a vacuum. If you do not fill your mind with positive thoughts, there is plenty of room for negative ones.

Use positive Affirmations whenever you think of them. You cannot have too many great thoughts. As a reminder to yourself to say positive thoughts often, you may pair the activity of saying Affirmations with another activity that you do on a regular basis. You may pair Affirmations with drinking coffee or water, with driving your car or taking a walk. A good time to remember Affirmations is anytime you are taking time out to relax. The more you practice Affirmations, the stronger a positive habit they become.

Affirmations are tools for us to build positive self-esteem, strength of character and peace of mind. Negative Affirmations or negative self-talk will create discord in our lives and disrupt relationships. Affirmations are meant to be positive and powerful forces in our lives.

As we take back control of our lives in this way, we move toward fulfilling our Purpose and living our Passion on a daily basis.

Guided Meditation
Rewarding Yourself for Growth

The purpose of this meditation is to reward your inner being for the growth steps you have already taken. As you prepare to reward yourself for all of the hard work that you have been doing, find yourself a quiet, gentle place where you will be undisturbed. Prepare yourself by relaxing your body into a comfortable chair, letting the chair take your full body weight as you melt deep into it.

With your eyes closed, breathe deeply, slowly and comfortably. Take an internal check of all your muscles groups and make certain that they are totally relaxed.

Once relaxed, begin to picture the color blue and let it fill all the spaces of your mind.

Change to the color green, a healing color, and let your mind and body relax even further.

Shift now to the color yellow and then to white as you prepare your mind to visualize yourself as an infant.

Begin by picturing yourself as an infant lying gently in your hands. In your own infant eyes, you see your future. Visualize all the glorious possibilities that lie before you. See all that you can be and ever will be. The future belongs to you in all its completeness.

Tell your infant self how much you love him or her. Embrace yourself and assure the child that all it ever wants to be or do is possible. Sense that it knows that you mean this with all of your heart.

Look into the glowing eyes of your infant and feel the incredible joy of being alive. Know that the universe loves you. Know that you are a child of the universe and you cannot fail; you can only thrive. Deeply sense that you love as much as you are loved. Know that love is always yours to give and receive whenever you offer yourself.

I'm not a frustrated mortal, but a child of God.
I'm not born to be a failure, but to reflect the qualities of God:
serenity, wisdom, vigor, love, hope and intelligence.

Beverly Allen's Affirmation

In this chapter we have discovered our life's mission. We could not have answered a more important question. When we are clear on why we are here, we can rise above the mundane aspects of our existence and be all that we are meant to be. From this point on it gets easier, for with this sense of inner direction, we cannot fail.

We can move through the world, move through our lives with grace, unafraid, releasing a constant stream of blessing and healing to everything and everyone around us. It is never too late to be a child!

Dawson Church, "Communing With the Spirit of Your Unborn Child"

Pathwalker: Larry Wilson

At age 29, Larry Wilson became the youngest lifetime member of the insurance industry's prestigious Million Dollar Round Table by selling over $15 million of insurance in five years. At age 30, Larry revolutionized the selling industry by developing his successful sales techniques into a series of training programs and starting Wilson Learning Corporation, a multinational training corporation located in Eden Prairie, Minnesota. In 1984, Larry Wilson started the Wilson Learning Interactive Technology Group in Santa Fe, New Mexico. He also opened the Pecos River Learning Center in the foothills of the Sangre de Cristo Mountains outside of Santa Fe. His programs are aimed at developing teamwork, managing change and developing empowered work groups.

I was impressed by Larry's sense of destiny and purpose. His energies are focused on helping people to be all that they can be and making the world a better place to live.

Discovering Purpose

"My real purpose in business and the driving force in my life is to help others become as much as they can be. At the Pecos River Learning Center where I reside and work, we have said that the Ranch's purpose is to help people discover their power, their courage, and their creativity, and to use this power in the service of creating a better world. So when I stop and get myself grounded, and try to remember the answer to the question, "Why am I here," that's what comes up for me.

"We are never given a purpose without the talents to bring it about. And it seems that I have been given talents to speak, to motivate, and to encourage. These talents are used in that purpose and these talents have been given to me. I don't take credit for them. They have been given to me and I hope that I am using them as well as I can.

"I think that I really discovered this when I had a face-to-face day with Abraham Maslow in the early sixties. He helped me understand my life as something bigger than success. I had already become the youngest lifetime member of the Million Dollar Round Table and I was trying to create a new training program based on what I had done. He helped me focus on something different and bigger than that. He asked rhetorically, 'What would it be like if you lived on an island with a 1000 people, all of whom were self-actualized?' He left us with the suggestion, 'Why don't you find that answer?'

"This challenge hit me like a thunderbolt. He brought forth the specific purpose that, I think, was already there in me. So although I was purportedly creating a sales training program, it was actually a Trojan Horse. I began to use the context sales training to move people to a higher level of discovery of who they were and why they were here, to connect them spiritually."

Joys, Blocks and Fulfillment

"Ego is a constant block to fulfilling our purpose," Wilson says. It is the part of us that believes that it is in charge, that it is the source of power, and that it is separate from everything else. The ego is so clever and smart and self-protective that it covers up the real and true self that we are, the miracle that we are. The ego is more oriented toward proving yourself than expressing your real self. I can't recall the number of times that my ego has gotten in the way of my purpose. I'm at my worst when I'm coming from my ego, my egocentric wish to control. At these times, I'm not really coming from the real true and loving part of me. At times like that I can always look back and see the ego in me purposely keeping me away from fulfilling my Purpose.

"Real Purpose puts you in an egoless state, in the sense that you commit yourself to something bigger than yourself. The seven deadly sins—pride, envy, lust, sloth, and so on—are never present when you are on Purpose. Ego tries to be in charge and keep you off Purpose."

"My greatest joy in life is my kids and my grandkids. The older I get the more I realize that. Second in line is loved ones that I have, and then my work. And I think I'm beginning to learn the love of God; I say that straight out, because when I look at my life backwards from the point of my death, I know how important that is.

"Ultimately, the only way we make a difference is by waking up the goodness in other people. We probably do that in ways that are different from what we think we've accomplished. We probably do that when we are being who we really are, rather than acting or coming from our ego. When I am coming from my true self, I'm closest to working as a tool of creation. It's that true self that people pick up, not the words, not the content, but the beingness. Each of us changes and adds to the planet to the degree that we are being who we really are.

"Many times, in little ways, I have wavered from my purpose. We waver when we begin to think with our ego, thinking that we are the cause of things, thinking that we are important because we are doing these great things all by ourselves. But if we are willing to listen carefully to what is inside, we discover that we're not happy in this state. It's been easier for me to stay on Purpose in my business life than it has been in my personal life. My divorce was a most painful thing for me, yet these life-crises are what force you to take a look at yourself, to put a mirror up to your face and say, 'What's really happening here?' These experiences alter my course of action, and I try a new and different way.

"There are several ways in which I keep myself on target each day. I try to be conscious of my feelings, of when I'm feeling inappropriately egotistical or inappropriately afraid–coming from fear. I've gotten better at being conscious of it. It's at that point that I'll make adjustments.

"Also, sometimes when I'm at my best I'll take some time to fully appreciate what I have. I haven't gotten this down perfectly; I've got a long way still to grow and to learn. I try to stop and ask myself some questions about life, to critique myself, to find alternate ways of looking at a situation. I go back in my past and think about times where I've learned from similar kinds of experiences, what I learned from the experience of the experience."

Faith and Vision

"Vision, to me, has always been a very important tool," Wilson goes on. "I think you allow a vision to come through you. I don't believe you will it to happen or make it up. If you allow yourself to be quiet, and just let yourself go, I think a vision will begin to form for you. This is very powerful truth in my life: I think that I have *caught* visions rather than *creating* them. There is a vision bigger than the scope of our individual lives; as tools of the Creator we are here to tune in to what that Creator wants us to be working on. I think that my whole experience–from selling insurance to starting Wilson Learning, and now to working at the Ranch–has all been part of a plan that is bigger than my own. I can't take credit for it; I can't say that I did that.

"I have great faith in being a part of something bigger than you are. Then, whatever is needed to carry out the purpose you're here for will be given to you. That tremendous faith has never disappointed me and has certainly helped guide me. So I think that faith is extremely important.

"I think that courage is extremely important; being able to go through something that you don't want to, especially when its easier not to! I've got a lot to learn about that one. Humor has been incredibly important and valuable. Learning to love ourselves and love others is vital.

"I think that the ultimate goal is to 'know thyself,' and listen to the wisdom that is in each one of us. Our ego tries to keep us away from this and to keep us busy. This does take time, but we must be willing to take time to hear the wisdom that is within each of us."

ADVENTURE
3
STEP

Dumping Your Blocks

Life, we have often been taught to believe, is limited. There is only so much time, energy, money and other resources to go around. Perhaps we even accept the notion that our talents are few, our energy low and our assets measured and finite.

Who says so? What reality is there to confirm these beliefs? Why do we feel these limitations are real, true and unconquerable? Our reality is what we create through our belief systems. Our belief systems are our windows to the world. They are developed primarily through cultural conditioning and practice. They represent collected sets of understandings in families, in neighborhoods, in cities and in nations.

Belief systems come from parents, siblings, peers, and playmates. As we are growing up, we develop a "self-view" based on the actions and reactions of those around us. The self-view is based on how we think others see us as we compete in the classroom and on the playground. It is affected by whether we are chosen first or last for the playground sports teams, and whether or not we come up with the correct answer in response to the teacher's question. In thousands of different ways, we begin to develop specific feelings about ourselves and our competencies that become part of an ongoing internal dialogue. This dialogue occurs as we take in all the information offered by various sources, process and shade it within our own matrix, and then

> *The happiness of your life depends on the quality of your thoughts; therefore guard accordingly!*
>
> Marcus Aurelius

create our own worldview from the hologram of this information. The die is cast from early childhood as our worldview fills with preconceptions, some of which remain with us when they are no longer relevant or useful!

A study by Shelley E. Taylor, Ph.D., of UCLA and Jonathon D. Brown, Ph.D., of Southern Methodist University concluded that "well-being virtually depends on the illusions of overly positive self-evaluations, exaggerated perceptions of control or mastery and unrealistic optimism." In other words, truly emotionally healthy, caring, content and productive people are able to filter negative information and orient only to positive, strengthening information. They are able to protect themselves from the effects of adversity by choosing to focus on the positive.

The view of ourselves that we held when we were seven years old may be managing our lives right now, regardless of what age we are. Our successes, our accomplishments, all the joyful events of our lives, may be denied or overridden if we are trapped by a sense of inadequacy as human beings. The truly "original sin" is that which cripples us with self-doubt and feelings of inadequacy. We felt that Mom liked our sister better. We were left to sit in a corner when our best friend was asked to dance. We were the last player chosen for the neighborhood baseball team. As the seven-year-old inside us cries, the adult in us feels like a victim of the past, unable to cope with the stresses and strains of the present.

Now here's the good news: it doesn't always have to be this way! What happened to us before is past; even what happened a second ago is gone. The past does not control the future unless we let it. *Now* is all we have. *Now* is the only moment that is important to us and to others. The choice is uniquely ours. If we accept false limitations, we make them what we are because that is how we behave. The decisions that we make in the present are all that really count. In the end, we must choose to be either who we are or less than who we are–so why not commit ourselves to life and growth!

Growth always requires a leap off the high diving board of life. Leaping into something "out there" that seems amorphous, unknown and unknowable demands absolute faith. But with a solid grasp of our own Purpose, we have a stable inner reality as a starting point. And the payoff for making the leap to growth is incredible, for we experience

---

Beliefs will vary, but life is one.

Bill Bahan

places we had only dreamed of before, far beyond our previous existence. In taking the leap, or in taking just one small step forward, we change dramatically. If you look back, you will clearly see that the leaps or risks in your life have always been the moments of greatest growth.

Take just a moment to review the book of your life, remembering all the chapters in detail. Recall the times when you dared, when you stepped off a comfortable place into what you called the unknown. Because we are somewhat reluctant to take these steps, it usually requires some stimulus to push us. In fact, we are often driven to change our behavior by situations or circumstances so adverse or uncomfortable that we simply can't stand them anymore.

Many people remain blocked because the discomfort is all they have and it represents a kind of comfort of its own. It is the known. The difficult situations these people choose become their traps rather than their challenges. All of their energies become invested in survival and problem-solving. Since so much energy is devoted to hanging on, it becomes a goal and focus of its own, and becomes the limiting factor that prevents growth.

The Thrill of Courage

I remember clearly a time when I was choosing against myself and against the situation. I was in a job that did not allow me to use my talents to the best of my ability. It was an uncomfortable situation, to say the least, filled with politics, intrigue, and frustration, but...it was secure. I kept telling myself I should resign and find a job that would give me joy, and I kept putting it off. Finally circumstances got so bad that I was forced to see the cost of staying with a terrible job that was secure versus taking the leap and trying something new. I took the plunge, left and began looking for a new job.

The position that followed was one of the greatest experiences of my life. It paid less financially, yet it paid more satisfaction than I had ever received before. The new job and new people were instrumental in changing my life, and I believe I was a positive force in many of their lives. This job also led to opportunities that I would never have

---

The future is the sum of all the instants we create. It is by being light in these present moments that we shed light into the future.

Dawson Church, "Communing with the Spirit of Your Unborn Child"

found in the other position. The universe watches out for us, even when we are stubborn.

Marlene Bennett, M.A., consultant, speaker and author, tells the following story in her forthcoming book, *Living Life through Illness and Disease.* "Living life is like a mountain. You can go around the mountain, you can go over the mountain, or you can cut straight through the mountain. Cutting through the mountain is indeed the shortest route, but also the most difficult.

"I apparently decided to cut through when at the age of 43, I was diagnosed as having non-Hodgkins lymphoma. To use the word 'cancer' was synonymous with death and I quickly began planning my own. Subjecting my children and elderly mother to the emotional and financial drain of this incurable disease was unthinkable to me. But God is ever so merciful, for as I was deeply involved in my death plan, sleep took over. When I awoke the course of my life was forever changed.

"As I turned my head, I saw a magnificent yellow rose lying on my tear-dampened pillow. Gazing at its beauty, I vaguely began to recall some of the words and ideas from the song, *"The Rose:"* love is like a seed, buried under the snow. With the spring comes the warmth of the sun, and the seed grows and eventually becomes a rose. That was me! I was the seed that had been buried by fear, anger, frustration. My spirit was lying dormant. My mind began racing with so many thoughts. Hadn't I been recently experiencing the spring of my life? I had recently begun a new career with a consulting firm and was speaking to hundreds of people. My divorce was final and the wounds were healing.

"As these thoughts filled my mind, my spirit exploded within me and I knew I could not die. I was just beginning to push through, like the seed. I couldn't die now because I wasn't a rose yet! I felt a joy, an aliveness that I'd never felt before. And so I began my journey through the mountain to self-awakening.

"I began reading every book I could get my hands on that dealt with cures. *Getting Well Again* was the most significant one, for it helped me understand that I had indeed played a part in bringing the cancer to myself. It clearly stated that if I had assisted in bringing the disease to myself, I could play a strong and powerful role in getting rid of it.

There's a divinity that shapes our ends,
Rough-hew them how we will.

William Shakespeare

"During three surgeries and chemotherapy, I turned to counseling and to my family and friends. When I lost all of my hair, I was devastated, but I turned to laughter as I modeled outrageous wigs. Tumors returned two to three months after treatments, I felt deep despair, but my higher self always provided the next step....My soul spoke to me of life, not death.

"I continued to work as a speaker and trainer, I dated, I traveled, I raised my two children and cared for my mother. I never felt special or courageous. I just did what I had to do each day. I cried and I prayed for tomorrow. I allowed myself to attend and experience many seminars which helped me release my creativity. Dancing and singing expanded my sense of freedom while the Indian Sweat Lodge pushed me to the limits of my fears.

"I just kept living life–one day at at time–one moment at a time. I kept learning, questioning, praying, meditating and changing my life-style. My family loved me and supported all my efforts. My friends were always with me. I was on my journey alone, but I was not lonely. Toward the end of my seventh year, I married a man who is love personified. So here I am today, almost a year tumor-free and still in the process of becoming what I am–a magnificent rose!"

Each act of courage is unique and personal. My courage and yours are demonstrated differently in response to our life's challenges. The important thing is that we face these challenges and learn from them rather than fleeing, freezing in fear or–worst of all–attacking others. Our challenges are gifts that allow us to grow. Our spirits grow more during our times of challenge than they do during the easy times.

Exercise
Great Courage

All of us in our lives have had moments when we demonstrated great courage, times when we took a chance and changed our lives. We may have shown great courage when we put our own needs aside for the moment and helped someone else, or let go of something or someone because the time had come.

Obstacles are those frightful things you see
When you take your eyes off your goals.

Anonymous

Take a moment to record a time when you demonstrated great courage in your life. Once you have recorded this information you discover just how much courage and power you actually have. This courage is available to you every single moment of your life and you can have access to it whenever you are shaky or uncertain. For example:

I demonstrated great courage when I...
> jumped out of an airplane
> got married
> moved to a foreign country
> gave up a good job for a new adventure

Your list: I demonstrated great courage when I...

> drove over pole in Gerry's car.
> sent letter to Ton
> fought for Shauna
> challenged staff over Les arts work

How did you feel?
For example:
> elated
> scared
> energized
> excited
> joyful
> strong

Your List: I felt...

> worried that I was at fault & later proud
> anxious — as if I sh'd'nt have
> happy but "contained" of fears
> confused & troubled, then relieved

What difficulties did you have to overcome?
For example:
    Fear of change and the unknown
    People trying to discourage me
    Fear of death
    Lack of money

Your List:
Difficulties that I had to overcome were:

unknown, responsibility
" possible disappointment?
going @ far " → hurting S.
talking control "

What strengths and resources have I utilized?
For example:
    Positive thinking
    Good friends
    Remembering past successes
    Fascination for change
    Willingness to risk
    Willingness to take the bad with the good
    Ability to anticipate the future and make relevant plans
    Ability to have fun

Your List:
The resources and strengths that I utilized were...

auto. pilot — self-confidence
bon aisé : que sera sera : my talent
reason, cool-headedness
obstinancy, reasoning, cunning

You have just identified your moment of great courage. Congratulations! All of us have resources that we are not aware of. Becoming conscious of just how strong we are gives us the power of that courage if we start to fall into negative thinking. When we remember that we have already demonstrated great courage, we know that we can do it again. Our courage is always there when we need it. It will not fail us if we tap into it. Courage is a part of who we are, it exists to reinforce our expression of Purpose and Passion.

Blocks to Success

In order to tap into our courage we sometimes need to release our blocks. *Blocks are learned fears.* We have learned them through all the negative experiences we have had throughout our years. However, since they have been learned, they can be unlearned. We can discover the immense personal freedom that springs from releasing our blocks.

Let's investigate the types of things that become blocks for us. Some of the most typical ones are:

Typical Blocks:
    Saying "I can't" be perfect.
    Worrying about events that have not yet happened
    Fearing failure
    Fearing change —growing incapable/older
    Guilt
    Looking at the physical aspects of life and seeing limits
    Willpower

The diagram on the next page demonstrates the hub of our fears. Each part of the chart includes one of the blocks to success and the way to release that block. As we identify the blocks and what generates them we will also describe and practice the way to release them.

Saying "I Can't" as a Block

Along the paths of our life, we develop self-concepts that are not compatible with growth and self-actualization. Our self-view becomes narrow, limiting, and negatively arrogant. We tell ourselves we can't, when we mean we won't, while the reality is that we can. Henry Ford said this best: "If you think you can, you're right! If you think you can't, you're also right!"

We decide fairly early in life what we will and will not allow ourselves to accomplish, and then we begin to believe that these limits are external. We simply refuse to accept that these are self-imposed limits. If we try and do not succeed, we call it "failure" rather than "growth through learning." We become fearful, creating a self-concept derived from our fears rather than our strengths. We act as if we could not live without approval, even from people we don't like. The fear of disapproval becomes a driving force determining what we try and what we decide we can't try. When you say "I can't" you exchange who you truly are for what you believe others want. And because you never really know what they want, you lose who you are.

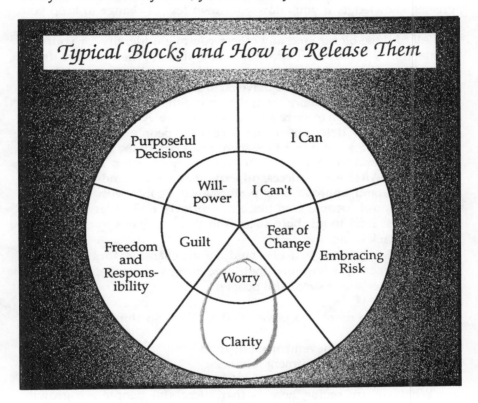

Success, Failure and Growth

How does saying "I can't" lead to fear of failure? Deciding you can't do something creates failure because we view failure as an ending rather than a beginning. Somehow failure becomes a judgment of unworthiness, which leads to a sense of lowered self-esteem. After all, if we can't accomplish something, what are we worth? Some people, especially the ones with a strong business and career orientation, tie their whole sense of accomplishment into producing results on the job. If things don't work out as planned, the feeling of failure poisons all other aspects of the person's life.

The reality of growth means that as we attempt new things, they will happen the way we envision them sometimes, and other times they won't. There is no reason to believe that one outcome, the one we call "failure," is any less useful in our growth than the one we call "success." After all, we learn through doing. If we don't do, we don't learn. If we don't learn, we don't ever do better. Activity and evaluation of that activity matures and seasons us. It awakens us to greater knowledge. If you allow your own fear of change to keep you from that joyful experience, you allow the block to continue.

All of these blocks, and any others you might identify for yourself, create limits for us that are not really there. When we are truly committed to something, there are no blocks or limitations. We can break through the barriers and move on to success.

Successful people more often than not either started with a strong internal belief system or were able to develop one. A 1985 study done by Anghel Velickov determined that successful people with an internal locus of control, a sense that they themselves determine the outcome of their life, tend to repeat their achievement after a successful experience. After an unsuccessful experience, they tend to intensify their efforts and improve their performance. People with an external locus of control (people who place control over their lives "out there" with others) tend to attribute success in their activities to chance and failure to lack of ability.

David McClelland, in a 1986 study of the characteristics of successful entrepreneurs, determined that three groups of competencies were more characteristic of successful people:

1. They are more proactive—that is, they do things before they have to;
2. They have achievement motivation.
3. They have a commitment to others.

What we are seeing here is that successful people see growth opportunities where unsuccessful people see simply problems or stumbling blocks. It starts as a matter of interpretation and ends with a way of life. It's always our choice.

There is nothing either good or bad, but thinking makes it so.

William Shakespeare

Exercise
Limitations and Resources

To help us let go of our blocks or limitations we will create two pertinent lists. The first is a list of limitations and the second is a list of resources.

1. LIST OF LIMITATIONS:

Examples:
    not enough money
    too fat
    too old
    not smart enough
    no experience
    no energy

misuse of intuit?

Your List:

weak physically — concentrate on energy meridians
slow logic — appreciate details
spread thin — enjoy the diff. moments
poor speaking — can see the contrasts work on breathing
unable @ dev. deep relatships — outpoor emot's

LIST OF RESOURCES:

Examples:
    good physical health
    education
    training
    good communication skills
    experience

Show me what you avoid, and I will show you your internal genius.

Alyce Cornyn-Selby, "Procrastinator's Success Kit"

Your List:

creative elemts
lateral thinkg
unusual experiences
intit

As you review these lists, compare the limitations list with the list of resources that you used when you demonstrated great courage. Drop from your list any limitations that no longer seem realistic. Also drop from your limitations list any limitations that conflict with your resources.

Example: I may not have the experience yet for this job or career, but I have experience in a similar field or experience as a quick learner.

When I started as a corporate trainer I had never done that job before, but I had been a manager, I had taught in universities and I had done considerable consulting with the business community. I was able to combine and transfer skills. Many corporate trainers have never taught formally before; they transfer other teaching skills, like training people on the job.

If you find any remaining limitations on your list, or if you find that certain ones rear their ugly heads like Medusa to blind you and kill your strength, go one step further to deny them any power over you.

Take each item on the limitations list that continues to give you trouble and picture it being killed off in some way that pleases you. For example, you might picture a great blob covering it over and absorbing it. Then send the great blob out into space. Or you may picture the limitation being burned at the stake. You may picture the limitation being put into a time capsule that will not be opened until the year 2020 when we no longer give any power to negative thinking. You may just take a black pen and wipe it out!

Have some fun with this; use a little humor. You may even design a collage of limitations, which you paint over with the word "junk." By using humor with the list of limitations, you can render them powerless. Limitations tend to be so humorless that they cannot withstand joyousness, just as certain bacteria cannot tolerate heat or cold.

Fear of Change as a Block

The fear of change acts as a block for us when we stay with the familiar and known, even when it no longer suits us, or when it hurts, constricts or bores us. The known discomfort, understood, broken in, like a comfortable shoe, feels right and fits in with our life. Old ways are like old acquaintances: we know what to expect, how to act, no matter that it may not bring happiness.

Who can really blame us for wanting to hang on to something comfortable. Isn't that natural? Yes, it is understandable, but no, it is definitely not natural. In fact, by resisting change because of a fear of making mistakes, we become rigid rather than naturally resilient. The fear associated with resistance leads to lack of harmony, illness, and eventually rigor mortis. To release fear is to find freedom.

Remember when you were a child learning to walk confidently? You got into everything! There wasn't any barrier, whether the side of the crib or furniture many times bigger than you, that you didn't feel was totally conquerable, within your reach if you just tried. You didn't know that you "shouldn't" learn through trial and error. So you did! You fell many times, but simply pulled yourself up and started over again.

Learning is a joy when we understand the principles. Because we are creatures of habit and conformity, social creatures, we tend to resist change without even realizing it. Being creatures of habit helps us in many ways. Imagine if you had to give the same concentration to your driving habits as you did when you were first learning. You would be totally exhausted before you even got to work.

But this conformity works against us when we are faced with a change in lifestyle. Many changes have occurred in our great corporations due to changes in consumer expectations and in the world market. Jobs have disappeared, new jobs have been created. The survivors are people who are able to adjust to change quickly and relatively easily. Those who become immobilized with fear or who become bitter and angry do not survive. One thing that helps us through change is a sense of control over our destiny. When we ourselves initiate the change, or when we can see the opportunities rather than the loss in a change, we regain control over our own lives.

Viktor Frankl made the following observation: "We who lived in concentration camps can remember the men who walked through the huts comforting others, giving away their last piece of bread. They may have been few in number, but they offer sufficient proof that everything can be taken from a man but one thing: the last of the human freedoms—to choose one's attitude in any given set of circumstances, to choose one's own way."

Exercise
The Profit and Loss Statement

In this exercise we practice taking control over our lives by seeing the gains rather than the losses in change. First, on the loss statement, list all of the losses you anticipate by making a change in your life, either in your career or your lifestyle. Following that, on the profit statement, list all the gains you anticipate by making this change.

LOSS STATEMENT:

_____

_____

_____

_____

_____

PROFIT STATEMENT:

_____

_____

_____

_____

_____

X_____

Return to the list of losses. After each one, ask yourself the following questions:

Is it really true that I will lose this?

If I do lose this, will it be so bad?

If I lose this, what will I gain?

Will losing this make me a better or a worse person?

Now add one extra gain to your list on the line marked with a big X. The X factor is the unknown, the gains that might be quite out of your ability to foresee. For example, by changing jobs you might meet a new person with whom you form a new and successful business partnership. You might fall in love with a customer you meet through your new job. All kinds of things might happen that would never have occurred had you not put yourself in fortune's way. Have fun with this. It is called serendipity and is the "science" of allowing joy, humor, excitement and new horizons to enter your life.

Compare your gains and losses. What this information tells you is that each change contains both gains and losses. As change is inevitable, it is to our advantage to learn how to manage change to enhance the gains in our lives at the same time that we let go of the losses.

Worry as a Block

Sometimes we block ourselves by worrying about tomorrow. We become prisoners of time. We worry about money as if it were a limited resource. We look at our lives and don't see enough "stuff": material possessions, talents, education, experience, health, and energy. We say things like "I'm too fat, too old, too tired, too sick, too poor." However, there is a huge luxury tax on worry: it costs us today! Our entire energy ration is spent in "limited resource thinking," which, of course, is non-productive. Looking at the physical aspects of life and seeing limitation is a serious block. Sayings like those on the list below are a sure road to missing our real potential.

Examples:
I come from a poor family.
Nobody in my family has ever taken risks.
People are against me.
It takes money to make money.
I don't have enough education.
I don't have enough time.

These statements sap energy rather than create it.

Our belief in limits is dramatically brought to mind by the example of a cancer patient treated by Dr. Bruno Klopfer in 1957. Dr. Klopfer was treating a man with severe lymphosarcoma. He had very large tumors, about the size of tennis balls, clustered on his neck, groin, abdomen, chest and armpits. His thoracic lymph duct was swollen closed and had to be drained of fluid each day. His spleen and liver were enormously enlarged, he had to be given oxygen to breathe and he was in great pain.

The patient, Mr. Wright, had great hope even in his desperation. He had heard of an experimental drug called Krebiozen, which was considered by its advocates to be the "miracle cure" for cancer. Although he did not qualify for the experimental drug program because he did not have a life expectancy of at least three to six months, he begged to be included in the study. Dr. Klopfer decided to give him one injection on Friday as he was not expected to live until Monday anyway.

After a single dose, the man's cancerous masses were half their original size. This was far more rapid regression than could be expected with conventional radiation therapy. The man had been feverish, weak and unable to get out of bed. Now he was walking around the ward, talking and laughing with people. He was cheerful, happy and energetic! Dr. Klopfer was amazed, as a single injection of Krebiozen could not have caused this incredible response.

Following this phenomenon, Dr. Klopfer decided to investigate this situation by continuing the treatment. Mr. Wright received injections of the drug three times a week, and within ten days he was released from the hospital. Virtually all symptoms of his cancer had disappeared. Mr. Wright returned to his normal activities and even returned to piloting his own plane.

During the next two months conflicting reports regarding the drug Krebiozen began to surface. The testing clinics reported no significant results. Mr. Wright became disturbed by the reports and began to lose faith and hope. Dr. Klopfer decided to explore what was really happening with his patient. He told Mr. Wright that Krebiozen was a very promising treatment, but that the first shipments had deteriorated rapidly in the bottles. He informed him that a new shipment of a super refined version of the drug would be arriving the next day.

Mr. Wright had become ill again when he heard the negative reports on Krebiozen. However, when he heard the news of the new form of the drug, he again became optimistic and was anxious to start treatment. Dr. Klopfer built positive anticipation in his patient by telling him that the delivery date had been pushed back. By the time the drug "arrived," Mr. Wright was extremely excited and anxious to begin treatment. What he actually received from Dr. Klopfer was sterile water, as there was actually no new form of the serum. Mr. Wright's recovery the second time was more dramatic than the first. His tumors disappeared, the fluid in his chest vanished, he became ambulatory and again went back to piloting his own plane. He was the picture of health. Dr. Klopfer continued the sterile water "treatments" and Mr. Wright remained symptom-free for over two months.

After two months the AMA announced that Krebiozen was a worthless drug in the treatment of cancer. Within a few days of reading this report, Mr. Wright was dead. Before he lost his life, he lost his faith!

It can be said with certainty that what we tell ourselves is true for us. If we send ourselves messages that say that life is wonderful and fulfilling, it is. If we concentrate on what we lack rather than what we have, we will continue to live without.

The "placebo effect" described in the behavior of Dr. Klopfer's patient has been demonstrated in a variety of physical and psychological disorders. Dr. Henry Beecher, a noted Harvard anesthesiologist, investigated the results of fifteen studies involving 1,082 patients. These patients suffered from a variety of medical problems including pain from wounds, pain from surgery, coughs, headaches and anxiety. The patients experienced relief even when placebos were used instead of regular medication.

When I worked at a District Hospital in Malaysia, the doctors frequently used sterile water shots for people with minor colds and flu. Some patients came too frequently for drug treatment and the doctors were fearful that if drugs were administered too often, the individuals would develop immunity. So when the illness was not serious and really only required rest, they injected sterile water and prescribed a day or two of bedrest to "let the medicine work." The treatment appeared to be very effective. Our beliefs about reality can and do change our physiological responses.

The placebo effect and other mental phenomena such as response to hypnotism have been linked directly to our self-talk. We are continually creating our lives through the belief systems that have been developing since birth. At this point in your life it may be time for a new view of the world and a new set of beliefs.

Exercise
Releasing Worry as a Block

List all of the situations that you have *improved* by worrying. Do not list those situations that you have improved by problem-solving or

> *Be not afraid of life.*
> *Believe that life is worth living,*
> *and your belief will help create the fact.*
>
> William James

creative thinking. List only those situations that you have improved by sweating, anxiety, frustration and out-and-out simple worry.

_____

_____

_____

I assume that this will be a very short list. Few of us are able to improve our lives through fruitless worry.

It is critical for us to know that it is well within our capability to change our thinking and thus change ourselves. It is primarily a question of responsibility. When we accept total responsibility for our lives, we give up blame and fear. We make the decision to be all that we can be. We "move and shake"; we cause the world around us to change. We emerge as eagles and soar to greater heights than we have ever reached before.

In preparation for the following meditation, make a list of all of your worries. List all of those compulsive little thoughts that nag at you day and night. All of those "things to do" and "what ifs and "shouldn't haves." After we make this list, we will dispose of it appropriately in our favorite place.

Worry Examples:
I must get the garage cleaned out.
I must get this project done.
I must get to the store.
I must catch up on my personal correspondence.
I must catch up on my business correspondence!

What if the stock market crashes again?
What if there's an earthquake?
What if I lose my job?
What if I get sick?
What if this deal doesn't go through?

I shouldn't have eaten that ice cream.
I shouldn't have confided in him.
I shouldn't have let the gas gauge get so low.
I shouldn't have turned in that report that way.
I shouldn't have yelled at her.

Guided Meditation
Releasing Worry

In preparation for this meditation, go to a quiet, peaceful place where you can relax undisturbed.

Take your list of worries with you. Once settled in your peaceful place, relax your body by breathing slowly, deeply and comfortably.

As you relax, begin to imagine the color blue filling the spaces of your mind.

Now fill your mind with the color green, a healing color.

As you continue to relax more and more, fill your mind with the color yellow and then fade it to the color white.

Return now to your special place. If you have forgotten the details, take a moment to reconstruct your favorite place in your mind.

As you relax in your favorite place review your list of worries.

You may find that there are worries on this list that teach you something important—like, are you always late? Do you avoid confrontation or create negative confrontations frequently? Do you tend to manage your time poorly? Do you procrastinate? Do you eat, drink or oversleep to relax? Many times our worries are really keys to necessary behavior changes. They sometimes show us the areas in our lives that are ripe for transformation.

As you look at your list see if there are any important lessons for you. If there are, write the lessons down on another piece of paper (the materials we need are always available in our favorite place).

Once you have written down the valuable lesson provided by the worry, take the original list and carry it to a bowl somewhere in your favorite place. If you are indoors, the bowl may be ceramic or metal. If you are outdoors, your bowl may be half a coconut or a hollowed out stone. Take your worry list and place it in the bowl. Tell it that you appreciate the lessons learned, but now you are releasing the negative parts of the worries to the wind. Burn the worry list in the bowl and speed it on its way.

You are now free of useless worry, but you have saved the essence of the lessons that the worries provided.

Continue to relax. Open your eyes and record the lessons learned from the worry list.

Examples:

I learned that I procrastinate.

I learned that I tend to avoid confrontation.

I learned that I worry about things over which I have no control.

Your list:

_____

_____

_____

_____

LIST OF SUCCESSES:
List the times that you have solved a problem by calming yourself down, looking at your options and opportunities and making a rational, positive decision.

_____

_____

_____

_____

_____

_____

This list demonstrates to you that you do in fact have the resources to solve your problems when you access your strengths. When you are fearful and begin to worry about change, refer back to this list and your Great Courage Exercise to give you the energy you need to reach your goals.

Guilt as a Block

One of the most popular learned blocks is guilt. Guilt often masquerades as caring for others, but it is really a way of avoiding responsibility for the now. It limits us by directing our energy in less risky ways. It keeps us trapped in old ways of thinking and old views of the world. Feeling guilty and acting on that allows us to put our lives on hold, to avoid new decisions and new pathways.

Have you ever caught yourself saying that you would like to change your life but you can't because you "owe" something to someone? We never owe our lives to anyone. We owe respect, caring, consideration, but not our lives. When I was a marriage counselor I frequently ran into married couples who had stayed together out of guilt, for the children, or because they owed each other something. But the guilt never changed their behavior toward each other. They still argued, hurt each other and strayed. It would have been better for them to feel less guilty and be more considerate of each other.

Guilt often stops us from looking at all the options we have; we turn some down because we would feel guilty doing them. I have a friend who feels quite guilty about how he treats the women in his life. The guilt, however, has never changed his behavior. He simply feels guilty and then continues in his old patterns, changing the women rather than himself. As a therapist I found this pattern in people over and over again. They would talk for hours about their guilt, but when it came time to look for ways to change, they were no longer interested.

The next exercise helps you to release your guilt either by simply letting it go or by rectifying the situations that are a source of guilt for you.

Exercise
Dumping Guilt

List all the things that you feel guilty about:

_____

_____

_____

_____

_____

_____

_____

At this point, either decide to release the guilt or make amends. Either choice is appropriate. Often when we release guilt we are able to act in a more loving and appropriate way.

Situations you will rectify or in which you will release guilt:

_____

_____

_____

_____

_____

_____

Guided Visualization Dumping Guilt

Go to your quiet place.

Relax by closing your eyes and breathing slowly, easily and comfortably.

Begin by picturing the color blue, then the color green, then yellow and finally fill your mind with the color white.

In your mind, take your guilt list to the city dump. It will cost you $20 to get in—dumping guilt isn't easy! Once inside the dump find a place where you can build a fire. Once the fire is burning brightly begin to tear your guilt list into strips and place them in the fire. As each strip of paper begins to burn, begin to laugh. Soon you will find yourself laughing hysterically as all your well worn guilt issues go up in smoke.

At the same time, picture the ghosts of those you have harmed laughing with you. As you laugh together you can forgive each other. It is difficult to stay angry at someone you are laughing with over a fire pit of guilt.

As you give and receive forgiveness around this fire, notice the sense of peace that surrounds all of you. When we feel guilty it is difficult to mend fences with others, but when we let go of guilt we are free to open ourselves up again.

Gently return to your body. Become aware of your breathing. Return to the present moment and notice how different your body feels now that you have released your guilt. Remember that the dump is always available to receive future guilt.

Guilt is an interesting phenomenon. It is one of the few blocks that we can use as a direct weapon of aggression at the same time that we use it for defense: "I'd come back to you and the children, but I feel so guilty. I can never make up for what I've done." Guilt can stand alone or be used in conjunction with other blocks like "I can"t." "I can't do that because I would feel so guilty!" What a terrific scam, until we consider the cost. It is important to make a conscious decision to let go of guilt, for everyone's sake.

Take your list of guilt items that you will rectify and copy them in your journal, if you have one, or onto a separate piece of paper. This is an *action list* and is not to be treated lightly. Check this list periodically, for example, once a week, to see if you are taking action.

Belief in Willpower as a Block

Willpower is a major self-limiting and self-abuse tool. Belief in willpower is typically verbalized with "shoulds," "woulds," and "musts," a clever way to convince ourselves that we can swim against the current. Believing in willpower is investing in limited thinking. You give away your power by doing what you think you "should." It is the exact opposite of being empowered from within by the act of living our Purpose and Passion.

Olympic pentathlon champion Marilyn King said, "People assume that it took a tremendous amount of willpower and discipline for me to achieve what I did on the Olympic level. While that may be true, I was never in touch with either willpower or discipline. What I did know was that every morning when I awoke, there was nothing I wanted more on the face of this earth than to be an Olympian. You don't have to have willpower to get out of bed to do your favorite thing. You bound out of bed. The fuel for sustaining that kind of intensity, for feeling empowered and energized, is desire!"

If Marilyn believed that willpower was enabling her to compete, then she would have allowed herself to feel guilty whenever there was the slightest wavering of purpose. Willpower tends to guide us into the self-recrimination of "Why didn't I?" "How could I have?" and "I really should have." This becomes a contest of strength between internal and external stimuli and what we believe we want.

If Marilyn King had pushed and forced a desire that wasn't truly there, she would not have achieved champion status. Instead, for her, it was only required that she look inward to see, feel and taste that grand Passion that became a legend. Each one of us can learn to extend our peak moments by tapping into our Passion. When we are in touch with the core of our desire, we develop inner strength and discover our hidden resources. Daily commitment to that purpose is what gives our life true meaning. When we are doing what we love, what we are committed to, we never need willpower.

The self-limiting blocks that we strew in our pathway remain as hurdles. It is only by giving up defensiveness, judgment and self-defeating attitudes that we are able to walk an open path, align ourselves with a higher goal, and avail ourselves of an abundant universe. If we cling to these negative qualities, we disintegrate with them. If we walk our path and live our passion, we abandon limits. We can stretch beyond the speed of light and the four-minute mile. We give up our limited views of ourselves for the greater picture of what we may be. We accept our own greater reality.

Exercise
Releasing Willpower as a Block

The best way to release willpower as a block is to do what we did with worry. List below all of the internal changes that you have made based purely on willpower or "should." Also list all of the habits you have changed, like overeating, nail-biting, coffee drinking, cigarette smoking, etc., by using willpower. Be scrupulously honest.

_____

_____

_____

As with worry, this list is most likely very short or non-existent. We think that we can just grit our teeth and do what we "should" do. But most times we really do what we "want" to do. It is more useful to use our strengths than to fight our weaknesses.

> *You cannot fail, you can only grow.*
>
> Thomas Edison

Guided Visualization
Releasing All Blocks

Go to your quiet, relaxing place. Prepare your mind for visualization by picturing the colors blue, green, yellow and white in succession to clear your mind of the extraneous.

Picture your most powerful block or blocks as giant black monoliths. These monoliths are 100 feet tall, black, shiny and carved with the name(s) of your block(s). Although they are powerful-looking and awesome, you recognize something about them that you did not realize before.

Each monolith is really alive with energy. Within this fearsome exterior lies a message of truth for you.

As you stand in front of your monoliths, one at a time, ask the energy of the monolith to reveal to you the inner truth of its message. This message is a gift to you from your higher self.

For example, within the monolith of fear is courage, the power to face fear and use it to motivate rather than enervate.

Within the monolith of saying "I can't" is the gift of saying "I can" and knowing that this is true. It also offers the gift of discernment, knowing what's right and not right for you.

Within the monolith of guilt may also be the gift of freedom. This means that we accept the gift of responsibility for our actions and the willingness to accept the consequences. It also may contain the gift of good intent, spurring us on to correct the injustices we have committed and sin no more.

Within the monolith of willpower may be the gift of being willing to make a decision and stick to it because we have agreed to and because it is right.

As you face each monolith and receive your gift of truth from it, you will notice that it telescopes down to the size of a few inches. At this point it is about the size of a small booklet. Each booklet has the gift inscribed inside it that that block held for you, the essence of the value of that former block. The books are yours to keep to remind you of your gifts.

Put each of the books somewhere in your body. If you received a book of love, you may wish to place it in your heart. Put the books wherever in your body feels right for you. Then gently return to the present moment. Become aware of your breathing. Notice how your body feels to have dumped the blocks it has been carrying around for so long.

We can have our excuses or we can have our success—but we can't have both. Each of us is faced with frustrations, fears, anxieties and stumbling blocks in our lives, but that doesn't mean that we need to let them stop us. What we do with these challenges is totally up to us. No one else ever has control over our thoughts or our behavior. It is our responsibility always whether we choose pain or Passion. It is our choice whether we choose anger and fear, or joy and positive experience.

The Great Courageous You

If you have done something once, you can do it again. Acts of great courage simply draw on the strengths and resources that we already have. The corollary is, if someone else has done something once, we can all do it. If someone has made a million dollars, so can we. If other people have started their own businesses, so can we. If someone else has climbed a mountain, so can we. If someone else has run across Canada with one leg, as did Terry Fox, then we certainly can with two legs. We can always do what we choose to do.

You have already identified yourself as a successful and courageous person. Where do you go from here? You go to places that acknowledge and reinforce this awareness that *you are already all that you need to be* and *you have all that you need to have.* You can take your blocks and turn them into gifts that further your Purpose. One effective way of doing this is to start each day in anticipation of living your Passion and fulfilling your Purpose. Some of the Affirmations that you can use to start your day are:

Life is a joy and a delight of peace, power and Passion.
I can do anything I choose to do.
I embrace change.
I accept success.
I see an unlimited life ahead of me.
I have the power of personal conviction.
I accept full responsibility for my life.

This book is really about creating your own good luck. It is about being willing to do good for yourself. When you do that, you will inevitably do good for others as well.

People are just about as happy as they make up their minds to be.

Abraham Lincoln

Pathwalker: Barbara Peace

Could the daughter of a poor mining/cowboy family in Arizona become the vice president of a prestigious bank? Would she then walk away from her job when it was no longer fulfilling and become a "starving artist?" For Barbara Peace, the answer was yes as she learned to follow her dreams.

Barbara Ellen Beach Peace was the seventh child of a hardworking Arizona cowboy and his wife. Born 20 years after the sixth child, Barbara came as a surprise to her parents. "I don't doubt that I was loved, but my parents were fast growing old and they were tired. They had not only raised their own children, but also my mother's five brothers and sisters. I was basically raised as an only child. My siblings were already grown by the time I was born.

"My father was an alcoholic who went on the wagon when I was about eight years old. He settled down for about 10 years and became a copper miner in Ajo, Arizona. My mother sold shoes in the company store, and worked as a seamstress evenings and Sundays. Despite our obvious lack of income–it was years later that I discovered that we were very poor–I was the best-dressed kid in school. Mom worked out a deal with a shoe salesman and I had a beautiful pair of matching cloth high-heeled shoes for every Sunday dress and every evening gown she made me.

"I was never denied material things; the company store operated on credit rather than cash. But words of affection or encouragement were in short supply. I was a very typical, nondescript, freckle-faced, wildly red-headed kid. As I grew into my teenage years Mother would allow me to wear only eyebrow pencil and a light lipstick. I looked odd–no eyes, only eyebrows and lips!

"I had several friends who were well-to-do. Their fathers were supervisors, or higher-paid technicians. I thought then, and still do today, that they were beautiful. I was constantly amazed that they allowed me entrance to their group. I even made the pom-pom squad.

"I was very shy and spent a lot of time in my own company. I remember spending hours alone in the desert tree house I had built under an old palo verde tree. I wandered about the desert admiring all the colors God had painted in such an arid land. I would sit quietly for hours and watch the desert come alive with all types of creatures, big and small. I would dream wondrous things–that I would marry a handsome man, live in a beautiful home and have four children. I would *not* be a mother who worked. I would be at home painting, and have fresh-baked cookies and milk for my children every day. I worried about my own mom. I worried about how hard she worked at home sewing for me and others. I worried about her being alone and lonely when dad worked shift work.

"I was given no rules by my parents and I never had to ask permission to do anything. I belonged to church and social groups like the Rainbow Girls and Job's Daughters. I attended church functions, but I spent every other minute at home watching mom sew and dreaming my dreams.

"I was always sick with something. I had severe ear problems, which resulted in a removal of the entire mastoid bone around my ear at age eighteen, just before my June third graduation and my June 14th wedding. My troubles with my hearing had just begun. I eventually became severely hearing impaired and have fought a lifelong battle with bone disease and equilibrium problems. I have no hearing in my right ear and only 55% in my left ear. I wear hearing aids and I am a great lip-reader. I must visit an ear specialist every other month for the rest of my life. The 'great ear battle' has taught me tenacity, given me compassion for others, and has helped me prove to myself that *anyone* can do *anything* she wants to do. We may have to struggle, but it's worth it.

"I married my childhood sweetheart when I was 18. We had been dating since I was 14. Roy was 18 and a freshman in college. My daughter Robin was born in 1962 and daughter Kriste in 1964. Six weeks after Kriste was born my mother was killed in an auto accident. Fourteen months later my father died, an alcoholic. The first two years of Kriste's life are missing for me. In my grief I blanked out the years after my parents' death.

"Roy and I moved to Phoenix after our marriage. He started teaching and I started out as a very lowly proof-machine operator at a local bank. In my early years of banking I hated the work. At one point I went to an employment agency and tried desperately to get work as a secretary or clerical worker. No one wanted an unskilled person. I stopped outside work temporarily when my second child was born in 1964."

Climbing the Career Ladder

"In 1969, finances forced me to work full-time," Barbara recalls. "I went back into banking as a secretary and new accounts clerk. I made a vow to be the best banker I could be. I had no set goals other than to

---

Stone walls do not a prison make
Nor iron bars a cage.

Richard Lovelace

learn as much as I could and be the best at what I did. I had no real secretarial training. I didn't know how to use an electric typewriter and I had absolutely no knowledge of how to open new accounts. But I learned.

"The job also required that I run a teller's window. I only had one week of training as a teller at another bank; now I was going to have to run a window for half a day. I assured them that I was an experienced teller. I spent every evening and weekend for months reading every banking manual I could get my hands on. I watched the tellers as they worked and kept learning.

"In June 1971 the operations officer was terminated and there was a shortage of qualified and experienced people to fill the job. I was made the first operations assistant in the bank. My job was to run the branch with assistance by phone from other offices. I had no experience in this area either, but I read and questioned and succeeded. In June 1972 I was promoted to assistant manager and operations officer of a larger branch, one that was in serious trouble. There were new things to learn, new puzzles to solve.

"In September of 1975 I was promoted again to a much larger office and in 1976 I became assistant vice president in charge of ten branch offices. In 1976 I was promoted again, to full vice president, and by 1981 I was responsible for the bank's statewide operations. In 1984 I was promoted again, to vice president and cashier of the fourth largest bank in the state of Arizona. I was the only woman vice president in this two-billion-dollar bank.

"It was a wonderful ride, but it began to take its toll on me personally, emotionally and physically. Despite all of the glory, success and the wonderful salary, something was missing from my life. The more successful I became, the deeper my unhappiness grew. My husband and I separated in 1981. I had never spent a night alone in my entire life and I was terrified. I was also afraid of losing the love of my family and my children because they all adored Roy. I felt that if they made a choice, it would surely be for him. The year of our separation was a nightmare, both physically and emotionally. Although I was quite ill, I worked every day. Two weeks after we were finally divorced, I went into hospital for what I thought would be a minor operation. I woke up three days later to discover that the doctors had performed a radical hysterectomy.

"Following my divorce the corporate world became my life. I still loved my husband and wished for a reconciliation, but this was not to be and he remarried. Although the next year was terrible, I found an inner strength that I did not know I possessed. I also discovered the true meaning of friendship, as my banking family cared for me. I sought counseling and found tremendous help in the writings of Robert Schuller, Richard Bach and Kahlil Gibran.

"My family still loved me and I discovered that I had the strength and ability to overcome tremendous odds. Because of my equilibrium problems, doctors had forbidden me to ride elevators, hike at an altitude of over 6,000 feet, or travel by aircraft or boat. I began to do these things anyway–and I did them alone. You can do whatever you want to do–you just have to try!

"I spent the next six years putting my life together again. I worked hard, played hard, traveled, and thought about painting. I had painted intermittently over the previous seven years and purchased many art books. I'd read and read about painting, but I just couldn't make the commitment to become an artist. After all, I was a highly respected career woman. I was well known, financially secure–and miserable! When another large bank purchased my bank in June of 1988, I took the plunge and resigned. I had high hopes for my art and thought about starting a gallery or business that would allow me to paint."

Making Changes

"At that point," says Barbara, "all of the old insecurities came dancing in with their favorite tunes: 'You can't, you're not smart enough, you're not talented enough,' and on and on. I spent eight miserable months listening to those little monsters and to my loving brothers and sisters. I almost regressed back through my previous seven years of growth. But one day a friend of mine said, 'Barb, seven months ago I visited with a lively, energetic lady of 46 going on 25, and today I see an old lady of 46 going on 85. When are you going to get smart!'

"I was furious with him! But his words helped me get my act together. I overcame the obstacles and moved to San Diego to start my own business as an executive recruiter. Did I take my new life and my new opportunities and start art school? No! I allowed the dancers in again.

"Six weeks into this wonderful new venture I realized that I was definitely on the wrong road. I signed up for art school 10 hours a week. This once-very-successful career woman now works part-time at a Mail Box store earning $4.75 an hour. And I have never been happier!

"I live very quietly. I read, paint, listen to music, and walk around the bay. I think and gaze out at the sea. I've made some wonderful new friends who visit occasionally. I write long letters to old friends. I have no desire to attend movies, parties, or engage in any group activity. I enjoy my solitude.

"My brothers and sisters don't consider my current lifestyle normal. They see me as a dilettante who gave up security and a high-paying job to live on a boat and 'play' at art. They are certain that I am into some kind of mid-life crisis.

"I welcome the quiet of the morning by sitting on my sun deck watching the sunrise. Random thoughts tiptoe through my mind as I drink my coffee. I wonder about the glory of God who made the sun shine. I review the day's agenda and think about life in general. I enjoy reading books by Robert Schuller, Leo Buscaglia, Richard Bach and Kahlil Gibran.

"The rest of my day includes my work at the Mail Box, small chores on the boat, painting, and dinner with friends at a local hotel bar. Evenings are for rest and relaxation. Tuesdays are set aside for art classes, as are Wednesday evenings and Saturday mornings. Sometimes I wander around taking photographs for future paintings. I have a companion, Bill, who is most supportive of my lifestyle. He and my daughters and their families are true and trusted friends, along with a beautiful sunrise, a flower, a child. These things cannot be bought–I am an extremely lucky and blessed individual.

"I am a very creative person, and my creativity has taken many forms and shapes. I have the ability to create my own world, to solve problems for myself and others, and to sew and paint. I know that I can do whatever I wish in this world. For years I denied this creativity. Today I acknowledge its existence and encourage its growth. My principal block was lack of confidence.

"At age 47 I have no 'I wish I had's...' I'd rather try and fail than look back and say 'I wish I had.' I generally rush in where angels fear to tread, yet I am incredibly lucky.

"I have always felt a sense of greater Purpose and I have struggled to identify it. It is so elusive that the search would sometimes drive me mad. I know that my Purpose is found in a combination of things, first of all my art, but also more than that. It has to do with people too. I have always been a caretaker, and I have often allowed this role to get in the way of what was best for me. I have now achieved a level of inner peace that allows me to accept each day and look for the blessings it has in store.

"I spent so many years unhappy. I know what that means and I know the struggle that it takes to change. I have seen the suffering that my unhappiness caused me and my loved ones. I believe that happiness is a state of mind. Happiness is being at peace with me. If I am satisfied with me, then my world is content and my relationships are good.

"In 1988 I made a six-figure income. To date, in my first few months as a full-time artist, I have grossed about $150.00–enough to buy art supplies. At some point I may begin to worry, and maybe I should be frightened. But I'm not: I know who I am and what I am capable of. There is no reason to fear. I am a happy person!

"To take a chance with life you must have faith in your own abilities. You must be willing to at least try to fulfill yourself, understanding that the road may be long and difficult, and you may need to sacrifice the old for the new. But if you discover yourself and your true Purpose in life, the rewards are immeasurable!"

The Power of Focus

Change is everything. Without change there is no growth, no meaning, no action toward our Purpose. Every living thing in the universe has Purpose. Earlier we used the example of the seed and the power of its Purpose. The genetic imprint in the seed attracts energy for the growth of the plant. The seed does not question its Purpose; it lives it, putting its whole existence into fulfilling that Purpose.

Even though the seed may light anywhere on earth, either in friendly or hostile environments, it will survive and thrive. The power of its Purpose is so strong that it will fulfill itself regardless of any apparent difficulties, for it has *focus*. Its resources are within, a part of its genetic structure. The direction for its existence is a critical part of what it is. This direction is built in, pre-planned and focused. So why do we human beings have such trouble finding and expressing our innate Purpose?

"It's easy for the seed," you may say. "It doesn't think." If it doesn't, all the better for it! An old Chinese saying states, "He who thinks little lives in felicity." As humans we have overthought our existence, and as a result we have created our own unhappiness and displeasure. We often use our thinking, imagining mechanisms to create images of distress and lack. We do not recognize our own value; we

> *Destiny is not a matter of chance,*
> *it is a matter of choice.*
>
> Anonymous

think of ourselves in negatives, without acceptance. We judge, challenge and reject. We do not check our thoughts to see if they are serving us; whether they are centered on our Purpose or whether they are diffused and random.

Focus is the critical element that allows us to get on with our work and our lives without going off in all directions and being distracted by the irrelevant. When we are focused we are in the *now*. We are peaceful and integrated; we cannot be thrown off course. When we are focused we are able to "let go" and live our Purpose; we listen to the still small voice inside that guides us to allow ourselves to be our best. To be like the seed is to live life in perfect tranquillity.

Purpose itself is like a magnet that attracts to it, from an abundant universe, all that it needs to allow itself to unfold. It draws from things unseen, unimagined by our limited thinking. It draws from totally unlimited resources. All that exists is formed from the substance of the universe. All things are created from this flow of substance, and we can at any time simply enter the stream of substance and draw out what we need according to the pictures we hold in our heads. You don't become a millionaire by making money. You make money because you have an existing mental picture of being a millionaire, so money comes to you. You become a great humanitarian by simply being a great humanitarian in the here and now. The pictures that we hold in our heads are our way of creating our reality. When we have the power of our Purpose behind us, and a clear focus on what that Purpose is, we cannot fail. When in focus, our thoughts are clear and aligned with our Purpose.

When we hold a magnifying glass in the sunlight, it brings the sun's rays, previously diffused, to a point of sharp focus. While those rays may have been warm in their diffused state, when focused they can start a fire. Our minds function in the same way. When our thoughts are in focus, they bring the power of our Purpose to bear on physical reality. With focus we can set our worlds alight.

Focus increases our energy exponentially. As with the magnifying glass or with the laser, energy is targeted and concentrated. It is the same energy, it is always there and we all have access to it. What is critical to its greater use or fullest potential is its focus, the process of targeting toward a goal. Focus means knowing what you want and going after it. It means not getting diffused by nay-sayers and can't-be-doners.

Scott Anderson enjoyed extraordinary early success as a magazine publisher. He started in the publishing business immediately after high school and by the time he was 25 years old he was editor and publisher of a trade magazine for locksmiths. As a result of a lot of hard work and a little luck he was doing very well financially. By age 31 he was able to fulfill a lifelong dream of owing his own magazine company.

Then he hit a block. Instead of being ecstatically happy, he questioned his success. It seemed as though everything had come too easily. Reflecting on this experience, he says, "I felt that somehow I was not worthy of all of the good things that were happening to me, that somehow I was getting by on a pass. After all, I was just a cooler repairman's son, truly middle-class. Why should I expect to do so much more than my dad?

"The result of this negative introspection was that I stopped believing in myself. My attitude began to hurt everything in my life: my business, my relationship with my wife and finally my health. I ended up with stress-induced panic attacks. (I recommend against them if you have the choice.) In essence, I turned my back on the power within me.

"My attitude so hurt my business that it declined and I was forced to sell out in April of 1986. The new owners chose to keep the company in Phoenix, with me in charge. I had a place to work–that is, until January 1987 when they moved the company back to Kentucky. My wife and I chose to stay in our adopted state of Arizona. For the first time in 15 years we were out of work and a little scared. My father died two days later.

"I was out of substantive work for over a year. Phoenix, Arizona, is not the Mecca of publishing and the few jobs available in publishing did not seem to be available to me. During this period we lost just about every possession we had, about $50,000 in cash, furniture and musical instruments; almost all of our material possessions. Finally, we lost the house that we had come to Arizona to build. It was a very, very difficult time.

"During this time we began to attend the local Unity church. My wife, Mary, thought that it would help brighten our outlook, our attitude. I don't like getting up early on Sunday, but I went anyway. I was struck by the words of the minister; I saw focus in the idea that there is a presence and a power that cares for us. The words touched me, reminding me of something that I knew to be true. In that moment my hope was reborn.

"Not long after that I finally got a job as a magazine publisher. It did not pay well, but it was a job! But something unusual happened. Although I tend to get along with everyone and I generally have an abiding respect for the person who signs my paychecks, I was unable to get along with my boss. I held on to this job, hating every minute of it. Then a better job came along, which involved running a new lock manufacturing company. It saved me from killing my boss.

"I plunged into my new job with relief. Three months later, the company closed down.

"Despite all the evidence to the contrary, I began to remember and really *feel* that I have a right to happiness and fulfillment. I knew that it was right that I not take just any job. I knew that I must find the job that was right for me. I got very quiet with myself, and inside I realized that I need not try to fit into someone else's idea of what I should be. The right career would come to fit me. If I held my focus, my inner knowing of what is right for me, it would come. I went inside to my strength and decided to not even reply to ads for marginal jobs. I knew that my good was coming.

"I asked my friends, ministers and many others to see me in light and to help find the right thing for me to do. And they did. When money got really tight after two more months of unemployment, I was inspired to call upon a friend, an owner of an ad agency, on the rare chance that he might need someone, even part-time, to help me make ends meet.

"He's a terrific guy, and he told me that I'd be perfect for his business but that they hadn't been hiring at all lately. He said that if I were to have a chance I would first have to pass muster with his partner, whom he described as much tougher than himself.

"Unbeknownst to me, the partner said no before even meeting me. But in deference to his friend, he met with me anyway. We talked for an hour and I walked out of his office with the job of national accounts manager and the enthusiastic appreciation of his partner.

"The work is such fun that I would do it as a hobby. I get to write and help produce television commercials. I get to record jingles in the recording studio. I get to work with customers. Most important of all, I get to work with the most loving, talented and creative souls I have ever had as colleagues. It is the best opportunity of my life. My bosses think I'm terrific and are thrilled to have me. It's the first time in a long time that I have had that appreciation expressed and I am at peace.

"Was it because I was such a great guy or because I have such sublime talent that I got the job? I judge myself to be pretty fair in both those categories, but it was the combination of my need of the right place to express my talents correctly and the agency's need of someone to do the job, to complete their family. Divine Order simply supplied the opportunity. My sincere belief in Divine Order brought me the perfect job at the perfect time. I chose real faith and was rewarded with a demonstration of Divine Law."

It wasn't the number of ads he answered that got Scott the perfect job. He certainly wasn't coming from desperation or self-doubt. Just the opposite: when he was doubting and desperate, he sank lower and lower. But when we know where we are going and all our energy is focused and concentrated toward that single goal, we are integrated within ourselves. We are directed and powerful.

All of our creativity, all of our capability to live our Passion, lies within us. All that is required is that we stop worrying for a while and pay attention to its guidance. All that we need to know or have is available to us when we stop, listen and accept. Albert Einstein, commenting on how his creative process worked, said that he was "not so much thinking as listening." We are the holders of the key that unlocks the storehouse of an abundant universe. The only requirement is that we turn the key. That key is our willingness to commit to life.

When we have identified our Purpose, we must then keep our *focus* on that Purpose in order to fulfill it. When we let go of the responsibility of keeping our Purpose in focus and guiding our energies toward it, we lose our way, lose our energy, and lose the joy of life. Focus puts power behind our Purpose.

Thomas Edison was a person with focus. He was one of our greatest inventors and he had incredible persistence. In October 1879, after thousands of experiments, Edison invented the first commercially practical light bulb. Edison never considered himself a failure and therefore he could not fail, even after numerous "unsuccessful" experiments. When asked by a reporter if he didn't feel like a failure after trying so many times to invent the light bulb, Edison replied that he now knew thousands of ways *not* to make a light bulb! Edison considered himself a genius and proved himself right. Just imagine if he had allowed his mind to brood over all his unsuccessful attempts; if he had dissipated his energy in misery over apparent failure. He probably would have become discouraged and given up.

Edison had the power of Purpose through focus. He was willing to take the responsibility to pursue his dreams and make them work. All of his energy and all of his joy went in the direction of accomplishment.

In the same way, it may take us a journey such as this one, and many false starts, before we get in touch with our Purpose. But when we are in touch with our Purpose, we can shine brightly as we allow the light within us to stream forth.

Understanding and using the power of our own focus is the most powerful personal tool that we will ever have. When we are clear on what we want and focus our thoughts and energies on what we want, we are virtually unstoppable. People do not raise themselves from poverty of resources, limited physical capabilities or less-than-obvious genius because they are different. They raise themselves to their highest capabilities because they *think differently*. They are willing to stretch themselves, to take risks, to go after what they want without wavering. These people do not stop at road-blocks. They see them as stepping-stones and move forward.

The next exercise will demonstrate to you, in an unusual way, the power of focus. When we are able to see the incredible power of personal focus, we are ready to use this power for our own good.

The Power of Focus

To demonstrate how the body responds to the mind's commands:

• Draw a cross on a piece of paper like this, or use the one in the book.

• Get a plumbing washer and hang it from a string so that it can hang freely. You can also use a necklace with a pendant that hangs freely.

• Place the paper in front of you on a table so that you can rest your elbow on the table and hang the washer and string over the middle of the cross. Hold the string so that the washer hangs about 1/4" to 1/2" above the center of the cross.

• Now, with the washer hanging over the paper, but not moving, *think* about the washer moving right to left across the target. Don't move a muscle. Just think about watching the washer move.

• Even though you were instructed not to move your hand, the washer seemed to moved without you!

• Try it again. This time, make doubly sure you are not moving a muscle. Imagine the washer moving up and down the vertical line on the target.

• The washer probably moved again, this time in a vertical direction.

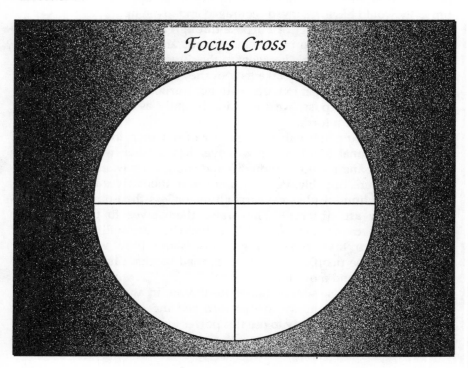

Focus Cross

What happened here? If you did not move your hand, why did the washer move across the target?

The answer is that *what we hold in our minds is what we create in our reality*. In other words, we create our own outcomes.

When we want something badly enough, when we are willing to put all of our energy toward that outcome, we will achieve our goal.

Lorrie Cade has a remarkable story of the power of focus. Through focus she was able to hold in her mind, over decades of time, what she wanted most in life. When Lorrie was seventeen years old she became pregnant by her high school sweetheart. The young man was unwilling to marry her and take on the responsibility of a family. Lorrie was left alone to make her decision. She was offered advice by her family and religious counselors, but everyone had a different opinion about what was right for her and the baby.

Confused about what would really be best for everyone, Lorrie prayed desperately, "Okay, God, tell me what to do. I don't think I can raise my baby, but I don't want to lose it either. I can't make this decision alone." Becoming more and more unhappy daily, she finally made a desperate plea, "God, please show me what I must do!" In a moment of peace and personal power, Lorrie suddenly knew what she must do. She knew that she was being told to give the baby up for adoption. Sad at the prospect of losing the child, she continued her prayer, "Oh, God, if it is right for me to do as you are telling me, then I must make a bargain with you. If I give this baby away, it is only with the understanding that I will see it again someday when I am able to. I want to be back together with my child." Lorrie had entered upon a decisive path, *without knowing how it could possibly work out*, she held the vision of reunion in her mind.

After the birth of the baby, Lorrie did not see the child but was told that she had a son. An attorney had arranged for the private adoption of the child to a couple who were members of a particular church that Lorrie had stipulated. The couple was paying the hospital bill and their name was accidentally put on Lorrie's hospital I.D. In this way she knew the name of the family and the church that they attended. Lorrie visited the church one Sunday and observed the adoptive parents with her baby. They did not know who she was, but she was pleased with what she saw.

Lorrie moved away and began to build her life. She had asked God to let her know if her son ever needed her. She promised to find him if he ever did. When her son was eleven years old, Lorrie awoke one night with the strong impression that her son needed her desperately. She was not well off financially at that time and was unable to get to him. She prayed fervently for his protection.

Seven years later, when her son was eighteen years old, Lorrie again received a strong message that she was desperately needed by her son. This time she was able to fly back to the state where her son was born and attempt to find his family. She went to their church that Sunday and saw the adoptive father. She approached him and introduced herself. She told him that she felt her son was in trouble and that she was offering her help at their discretion. She left her name and number with him and flew back home. She did not hear from the family.

Ironically, while she was home, the natural father of the boy returned to Lorrie's life. He said that he felt bad about deserting her eighteen years before and wanted to marry her now. She agreed to see him and build a friendship. The father asked Lorrie to contact their son and she agreed to write the adoptive parents a letter.

A week later she received a phone call from his adoptive mother. She was grateful to hear from Lorrie and anxious to get her help. When their son was eleven years old, his father took him camping and while on that trip told him that he was adopted. Prior to that time the boy had been a model son, but after finding out about his adoption he became a problem child. It was very traumatic for him and he was unable to contend with the idea of adoption.

At eighteen his adoptive mother had to ask him to leave her home because of his drug and alcohol use. She and her husband were divorced and the boy had been living with her. She was in emotional pain and so was her son.

She invited Lorrie to come to her home and meet her son if he was agreeable. The young man was thrilled at the prospect of meeting his birth mother, but he asked that he be given a few weeks so that he might get himself off the drugs and in better condition to meet the mother he had never seen. After a few weeks he called Lorrie and said that he could not wait any longer; he wanted to meet her as soon as possible.

Lorrie and her son spent two weeks together at his adoptive mother's home. He had greatly improved, and was recovering from his drug and alcohol use. When Lorrie first walked into the house her son grabbed her and hugged her until she could hardly breathe. Neither one wanted to let go for a long time. They talked all night long and well into the next day. They agreed to try everything possible to build a life together and help each other.

Following their meeting, Lorrie's son came to live with her. He is rebuilding his life and now has the benefit of two mothers and two fathers who care for him and love him. Lorrie and her son are building strong lives both independently and together. They are able to offer each other their strength and their commitment.

Lorrie focused on what she wanted: to be able to see her son again. She held that idea in her mind and put her full mental energy behind the outcome she desired. She could not see the details. She did not know exactly how it was going to happen with her apparently limited resources, she just knew that it *would* happen. She never wavered in the idea that she could make it happen, that she would be reunited with her son. She never let go of her faith in herself and her faith in that inner knowing. When we have focus we are empowered, and we unconsciously draw toward us those things necessary to our fulfillment.

Most of us have had times in our lives when we have been focused, when we have experienced the intensity of knowing exactly what we wanted and put all of our energy into reaching our goal. It is time to dig back into our memory banks and remember those times when we were clear on our goals and direct in our actions.

Exercise
Focusing

- Take a moment to get relaxed and comfortable.
- Allow yourself 15 or 20 minutes for this exercise.
- As you relax, go back in your mind to your special place, that favorite spot in which you can be fully you, where you can let your great self roam freely.
- After a few minutes in your special place, begin to recall times in your life when you knew exactly what you wanted and you put all of your intensity into those goals.
- Record the details of the event and then record the resources you drew on to stay focused and on target.
- Remember exactly how you accomplished your goal.
- Record your impressions in this book or in your personal journal.

Describe the experience of when you have stayed focused and on target:

_____

_____

_____

_____

_____

_____

What resources did you draw on?
I was able to stay on target because I:

_____

_____

_____

_____

_____

The personal skills that I use to get and stay focused are:

_____

_____

_____

_____

_____

Guided Visualization
Focusing

Go to your quiet, peaceful meditation place. Relax and focus your mind by visualizing the colors blue, green, yellow and white sequentially in your mind.

Breathe slowly, deeply and comfortably. Relax all of your muscles. Once you are relaxed and have turned your attention inward, return to your favorite place. Fill your mind with all of the wonderful things you love about your favorite place, the sights, sounds, smells and tastes.

In your favorite place you will find an empty space. In this empty space, begin to build a sculpture that represents focus to you. There are no guidelines here, anything goes. This is your picture of what focus looks like to you—it could be anything from a Star Wars *character to* Michelangelo's David, *from an abstract windmill to a sculptured starbeam. This sculpture belongs to you, it comes from your creativity. Take some care with this. It is your representation of your own focus. Shape it as a reminder to you to stay on focus. Whatever its shape, whenever you picture that sculpture in your mind, it should remind you of your supreme focus. Treat it with care and cherish it.*

Once you have put the finishing touches on your sculpture, imprint this image on your mind so that you will be reminded of it whenever you get off focus.

Become aware of your breathing once again, and holding the power of focus in your thoughts, bring your attention gently back into the room.

Experiences

One workshop participant reports on this visualization: "I found this exercise to be wonderfully creative. It gave me an opportunity to gently guide my inner self toward the creation of something special for me."

Another said, "I was amazed at what I came out with. My sculpture was made of light. It was alive with energy and did not hold one form. It is like the representation of the Holy Spirit for me, or the light energy that we are all supposedly made of. It gave me a sense of peace and total joy at the same time. I felt energized and elated."

With each exercise we access more and more of what is strongest and best in ourselves. As we work through our day-to-day responsibilities, we often forget what is most meaningful to us. We can sometimes get lost in "things to do" and in our fears. The more we practice identifying our strengths and building on them, the easier it will be to live out of the very best of who we are always.

Affirmations
Focusing

Write down an affirmation that sums up your focus for you. Make it short and sweet, a powerful statement of the intensity of your focus, so that you can call on it as a reminder in any moment that you feel yourself losing the sharp edge of your focus. You can build on the following examples, but don't follow them too closely, for each of your affirmations needs to be uniquely yours, tailored to your individual situation.

I am strong, focused, powerful.

Life is filled with meaning and wonder.

I know with total certainty that I am capable of reaching my goals and living my Purpose and my Passion.

I make every step I take bring me closer to my Purpose.

Nothing can shake my focus on my Purpose.

I focus the full Power of my Purpose in this moment, on this situation.

Your Focus Affirmation:

_____

_____

_____

_____

Remember to say your affirmations on a regular basis. To stay focused on the positive, we must practice the positive.

Pathwalker: Thea Alexander

Thea Alexander is an author, wife, mother and founder of the MACRO Society. She is the author of *2150 A.D.*, a classic in science fiction. The MACRO Society is dedicated to the development of personal responsibility for the future of our world and Thea is dedicated to advancing this philosophy.

Thea is warm, sincere and intelligent. She is able to draw you into her world while not disturbing yours. She shares her philosophy of life in a straightforward, quiet manner. There is a gentle firmness, a solid sense of self, coupled with a self-modulated joyousness. Rather than manifesting itself as exuberance, her happiness is apparent in her quiet sense of inner peace and self-mastery.

Thea is very far along her path and very conscious of the effects of her behavior. She knows where she needs to go in her development and is aware that life is a process and a series of lessons, opportunities and adventures.

Thea has two grown children, three ex-husbands and one current husband. Like many of us, she did not necessarily learn all of her lessons the first time! Her son Don is a creative and successful businessman, and her daughter Bonnie is a nurse.

On Purpose

"What I have *perceived* as my life Purpose has changed from time to time. For the first twenty years it was to grow up, be a wife and have babies, all of which I did. After attempting to deal with a husband who would not cooperate in my change and growth, I left the father of my children and pursued a different life Purpose.

"The second twenty years of my life were spent educating myself and supporting my two children. I was a very bright student and had been encouraged to go to college. My block was 'That's for rich kids.' I am from Small Town, USA. I didn't see how I could use Latin, algebra, and world history to clean house, can vegetables, and raise children. I dropped out of high school during my final year.

"After my divorce I moved to California to be with an older sister. Twenty minutes after my arrival she had me enrolled to finish high school. I took all of the required tests and completed the three courses required by California state law.

"One of my children got mononucleosis, and I had to return to my home state to get help with the medical bills. While I was gone, my name was submitted for a scholarship. I interviewed for the scholarship the day I returned to California and was awarded a scholarship to college.

"I received my B.A. from the University of Arizona in psychology, my master's from Gannon College in counseling and have done my doctoral work in counseling at Arizona State University. The most important thing, however, was that I began to realize how capable I am and how many abilities I have. I acknowledged my own capabilities for the first time and discovered that I was skilled in counseling.

"People often have no idea of their own value or their own life Purpose. My present life Purpose is to celebrate life, choosing happiness consistently and exposing other people to the fact that they too have a choice.

"I know that I must honor myself. When Thea is clear, at peace, and joyously content with what is; when Thea is living with great anticipation of what will be, then Thea can be the best that she is and the rest of the world can't help but benefit.

"I am a cell in the mind of God or, if you prefer, the macrocosm. If I keep the part of this universe that is Thea as shiny as possible and honor myself, I share my best with others and thus with the universe as a whole.

"Life circumstances make your Purpose clear. It is an inner knowing. I knew that *2150 A.D.* was meant to be, so I self-published. When it became an underground best-seller, a number of large publishing houses wanted the book. I could have made a bundle had I been willing to distort my truth to appeal to the masses. I wasn't. Eventually a publisher came along who understood the book's purpose and maintained its integrity as I maintained mine."

Blocks and Obstacles

"My own 'micro,' or narrow, perspective has been my major block," Thea says. "Narrow thinking cripples us. I saw lack of education as my block, and education as my expansion. When you are crippled in your body, you still have the opportunity to overcome through your thinking, but when you are narrow and crippled in your thinking, you are stuck. I was lucky: I started out so far down that the university required me to take 'dummy' English; my teacher in this course was very good, and expanded my horizons.

"Another block was my choice of husbands. One felt that he was the thinker and I was the doer, and said so. I stayed in that marriage, though my husband insisted that I be less than he.

"This revealed another block: lack of confidence. I now see negative thoughts as little people. I 'pat them on the popo' and send them off to meditate. I did the same thing with my children when they were small. If they became irritable, I would tell them lovingly to go off alone to their own room and come back as soon as they were better company.

"My greatest joy is the love that I give and the love that I receive. My husband, children, each person. Freedom comes when you 'unzip' yourself, when you bring yourself defenselessly forward and share yourself genuinely and consistently."

Living Your Purpose Helps Others

"I have received thousands of letters in response to my books," Thea continues. "I know from these letters that I have made a difference in people's lives. I've heard the terms 'micro' and 'Macro' thinking being used on television shows like *Saturday Night Live*. The most poignant letter was from a woman who wrote thanking me for saving her life. Her mother had encouraged her to read *2150 A.D.* prior to her vacation to California with her husband and young son. It was the last day of the trip and her little boy asked if he could say good-bye to the ocean. Her husband and child walked to the edge of the cliff and as they waved goodbye to the ocean, the ledge gave way. They both fell to their death. The young woman said that she would most certainly have followed them if she had not read *2150 A.D.* which gave her a broader, more macro perspective on this life." (Thea cried as she related this story, its clarity and emotion still deeply affecting her).

"The best thing that I have ever done for the universe is to clean up my own act and to live each hour of my life with the constant intent of choosing joy. The reward for joyful living was demonstrated on my forty-fifth birthday when I gave myself a party and invited a particular woman friend. She asked to bring another friend, and that friend brought a friend. That person turned out to be my present husband.

"I learned that love is definitely about letting go, about being able to say 'I love you, good-bye,' not rejecting, but speaking in a loving and caring way. Love means a genuine desire for your own best joy and that of the other person. It also means, in joyous anticipation of tomorrow, to say, 'From this moment on, I choose joy with or without a mate beside me.' "

Keeping on Target

"My PLM's (Poor Little Me's) get in the way sometimes. When that happens I deliberately take a more Macro perspective and laugh at myself for doing something so dumb as to choose the drama, the soap-opera part of life, when I could be choosing the fun part, the joy. I have a motto printed on the back of my card: 'I believe in the Macrocosmic oneness of all and in myself as a perfectly functioning aspect of that

Macrocosm.' I believe that I, and only I, have the honor and the power to determine, to design, and to alter whatever my daily life contains, for it is the result of my own thoughts.

"I believe that there are as many paths as there are people to walk them, and that each person is the best judge of which path she or he will most effectively walk at any given time. I seek the adventure of interaction with others, knowing that it is the classroom of my evolution. I joyously receive this and every day, knowing that it is the canvas upon which I am painting my life. I have the constant awareness of honoring myself and every other person on the face of the earth. I know that each of us (given, as tools, the life we have lived until now) is doing the very best we possibly can at this time in our lives. Though we may want tomorrow to be somewhat different, each and every one of us is 'perfect enough for today.'

"I had previously written a philosophy book, but I knew that if my purpose was to offer joy, to let people know they have a choice, I needed to present Macro philosophy in a manner which would be easy and fun for the average person to read and to understand. Science fiction seemed perfect, so *2150 A.D.* was born. I have a deep hunger or drive to ease the pain of modern man. In the past I used that as motivation to work. Now I use it to entertain myself and to have fun. My 'savior' role is now sporadic."

Perfect Enough for Today

"The way to improve the quality of your daily life is to clearly define, in writing, what you really want out of life. Put it down in the most specific terms possible: ALL of it, mental, emotional, spiritual and physical; today, next year, five years from now, twenty years from now. Reread, edit and live with it for two or three weeks. Revise it, then keep it open for revision–for the rest of your life. Having clearly defined what you want, you should then write down specific alternate possible paths to achieve those goals. You must be willing to apply yourself to one path.

"Equally important, you must be willing to *not* apply yourself to the other paths, to focus on that essential one. People decide to go in one direction–for example, to be a dentist–on one hand; but with the other hand they wish they were doing something else. If they wanted the other path, they'd be there! Accept the joy of the path you have chosen or choose a different one, but don't straddle the fence. Give your all to what you've chosen.

"Laugh a lot and when in doubt, embrace the kindest possible thought. Always remember that in spite of micro evidence to the contrary, everyone on the face of the earth is perfect enough for today."

The Decision to Act

What is the value of making a decision? When we make a clear decision to act on our Purpose, we affirm our willingness to live our lives rightly. When we live our Purpose, we live with total integrity in every moment of our lives. We begin living the totality of who we are rather than living the disconnected, scattered life that we have often called "normal."

As we discovered in our examination of our blocks, when we are dishonest with ourselves and others, we get hurt. It may not be the kind of hurt that we can identify immediately, but it is the kind of hurt that creates a continuous feeling of separation–a dull pain around the psyche. This dishonesty comes from fear, the fear that if we live our lives as we know we must, we will not be "happy," we will not have "fun," and we will not be "rich."

For example, many artists have believed that to follow their Passion for painting, sculpture, or craft meant that they must be poor but proud. And of course this is true–if we believe it is so. Picasso obviously felt differently; he became very wealthy through his art. What will happen if we were all to make a similar shift in our perspective toward the work we love most dearly?

> *If you do what you've always done,*
> *You'll get what you've always gotten.*
>
> Anonymous

The Leap to the Possible

When you accept your own worthiness, your great inner self allows you to make the best use of opportunities that arise. But when you focus on your limitations, when you judge yourself to be less than the fullness of who you are, you are certain to prove this true. You will get plenty of confirmation from others, because your "others" are mirrors. Each time you accept a low opinion or unfair criticism from another, you are simply reflecting your own low self-esteem. Ultimately, you cannot blame someone else for treating you badly if you treat yourself badly. It is vital that we take the responsibility for controlling our own lives.

Personal moral courage is a matter of choice, whether it is in service to ourselves or to others. It takes personal courage to eat an ice cream cone in front of others when you are overweight. They will be quick to judge, a reflection of your own self-judgment. It takes personal courage to fight the school board when you know you're right. The school might punish your child, a reflection of your own fears. It takes personal courage to defend someone else when others say, "Leave it alone, it's not your battle," or "Let *them* take care of it." They are reflecting your own willingness to let other people take responsibility for the world.

Each time you stand up for what you believe in you have made a choice. Each time you do not stand up for what you believe in you have also made a choice. In the book, *The Altruistic Personality: Rescuers of Jews in Nazi Germany* by Samuel and Pearl Oliner, we find that those who helped the Jews said they had no choice but to do what they did.

The fascinating thing, though, is that those who refused to help Jews when they could have also gave *exactly the same reason:* "they had no choice," since they wished to protect themselves and their families. We decide which path to take: we are making a choice every time we feel "we have no choice."

When we recognize and accept our Passion and our Purpose, others acknowledge us and align with us. A firm decision to follow our Passion is visible to others and life-changing for ourselves, for we make a commitment to consistently live from our inner conviction of value. This commitment brings peace.

The decision requires a leap of faith, a risk. For each of us the time must come when we decide to jump off the high-dive board of life and risk everything for the thrill of living fully.

Exercise
The Leap of Faith

Close your eyes and think back over the times in your life when you said to yourself, "Go for it!" Think of a particular time when you were faced with a choice of whether to take a big leap or refuse—and you jumped! Think of a decision you took to make your life all that it could be. Reflect on the feelings you experienced when you made that decision to risk. Did you feel exhilaration, excitement, high energy, tension?

With your eyes still closed, clear your mind of all other pictures by viewing the color spectrum from blue to green to red to yellow to white. When your mind is clear and calm, fill your mind with the picture of a large, deep swimming pool. At the deepest end of the pool there is a very high diving board, about 15 feet above the water.

Check out your body and make certain that all of your muscles are relaxed. Make sure that your breathing is slow and steady, and your mind restful. Picture yourself standing at the bottom of the diving board. As you look up and prepare to climb the ladder to the top, tell yourself how excited you are to be able to make this great leap. Look forward to the risk and the challenge.

Climb the ladder slowly. At every third step, pause and look around at the view. The scenery is beautiful, and as you climb higher and higher, the view becomes breathtaking. As you reach the top and stand ready to walk to the end of the diving board, take a long moment to turn 180 degrees and look at the glorious view of the world. Take a deep breath and check your body and your mind to make certain that you are calm and at peace.

Walk slowly to the end of the diving board. As you look down at the water, notice the thrill that runs through your body as you realize the risk involved. You will be sailing out into space; there will be no one with you. The way you hold your body, the way you enter the water, arms first or feet first, is totally up to you. You are in control of your behavior and you are responsible for how you accomplish this feat. The challenge is yours and the success will be yours.

Now go ahead and jump!

Notice how it feels to be in that eternal moment between diving board and water. Feel your body slipping through the air, staying calm and under control despite the fear.

Feel the temperature and pressure change as you enter the water, smoothly and gracefully. Notice how you feel after you break back up through the water. Feel the sun hitting your face as you surface. Feel the water roll off your face, your hair, your shoulders. Feel the surge of energy that courses through your body as you rise to the top of the water, swim to the edge and pull yourself up and out of the water.

Sit on the edge of the pool and take as much time as you like to bask in the glory of your success. Recall all the feelings you had while experiencing your climb to the top and walking toward the end. Appreciate yourself for having taken the dive.

Gently come back to the present moment, open your eyes and record in your journal the thoughts and emotions you noticed during this exercise.

As with the Great Courage Exercise, this exercise helps you to tap into that inner strength that fuels your growth and change. It gives you a sense of power over your life.

We all have the desire to make our lives fuller, more meaningful, more peaceful. To make the difference, we need to close the perceptual door to the room of "I can't" and open the door to the room of "I will." If we have opened a door only to discover a roomful of inadequacies, self-doubt, limitations, and false beliefs, we can decide to close that door and walk away. We can simply walk across the hall to the doorway to faith and self-acceptance. The perceptual door of "everything is possible" is the one we wish to enter and explore. We are never given dreams without also being given the talents to fulfill those dreams. We are never given challenges greater than our ability to meet them.

In this next exercise we learn to access that room of "I Can" whenever we need to.

Exercise
Accessing the Room of "I Can"

- Take a moment to close your eyes and relax. Breathe deeply and comfortably.
- Make a list in your mind of all the things that you can do. List all of your talents, skills and abilities.
- Now open your eyes and record this list. It will later serve as a reminder of your capabilities.

Examples:
> I can write.
> I can ski.
> I can teach.
> I can play freely with children.
> I can learn quickly.
> I can run.
> I can use this computer.

I can:

_____

_____

_____

_____

_____

_____

_____

If you are like most of us, your list may be relatively short when compared with the list of your *true* capabilities. In order to access all of your skills and competencies we will return to the place that holds all of your answers, your favorite place.

Guided Meditation
Entering the Door of "I Can"

Go to your quiet, restful place and relax your body.

Sit comfortably, breathe deeply and slowly, and gently focus on the colors, blue, green, yellow and white. Clear and rest your mind.

Once your mind is clear of the extraneous, begin to imagine your favorite place. Look around at all the familiar and wonderful scenes in your favorite place.

All at once, notice that there is a building that you have never seen before. It is of great interest to you. It may be a castle, a small rustic house, a mansion or a monastery. This house is your house. It contains all the rooms of your mind. As you enter your house and investigate what it looks like inside you notice a door marked I CAN.

Open the door and see all of the things inside. The walls of this room are covered with lists of the things you are able to do. Notice little details that you had forgotten. The number of skills, competencies and capabilities represented in this room is much larger than the list you made previously. There are so many details that you had forgotten, so many wonderful talents that you didn't even realize you had.

Enjoy this room for a long time, don't rush. Take in all of the information about your capabilities that this room offers you. Hold them in your mind and in your heart. With this information it would be difficult to feel inadequate again. In this room of I CAN you have the true knowledge of who you really are and what you CAN do!

When you have finished admiring all the wonderful things written on the walls, leave the room and close the door, secure in the knowledge that you can go back to it to reassure yourself of your capabilities any time.

Become aware of your breathing, and gently return your awareness to the place where you are sitting. Whenever you feel inadequate, go back to the room of I CAN.

Experiences

We are logical beings. It is useful to us to be able to back up our dreams with substantial data about our capabilities. What is important to know is that *our dreams are actually based on our capabilities and skills.* That is why so many people succeed when they follow their dreams. We all have so many more talents than we usually acknowledge. We tend to be like the man in the Bible: we bury our talents instead of using them.

Even in the face of seemingly impossible odds, dreams can be fulfilled. When we read the biographies of famous people—artists, religious leaders, entrepreneurs and humanitarians—we often discover that their Paths were not smooth nor their way made easy by others. Dr. Robert Schuller, minister of the Crystal Cathedral, entitled one of his books *Tough Times Don't Last, but Tough People Do.* I believe that. We are all strong, we just don't always want to be.

Pam Lontos, president of Lontos Sales and Motivation, Inc., and a former vice president of Shamrock Broadcasting, owned by Disney, started her growth process with quite a few boulders in the way. She was an extremely shy child who avoided speaking out in class, or any form of social interaction. As she grew to adulthood she earned money for her family by selling shoes. She did well, but with her new maturity came a responsibility she would have as soon avoided. Although her family praised her success, they also expected her to handle irate creditors and landlords.

"How I hated it," she relates in her book, *Don't Tell Me It's Impossible Until After I've Already Done It.* Pam tells the story of a woman who went from a domineering father to a domineering husband: "Pessimism bound me, holding me back from virtually everything I wanted to do....I was so filled with negative thoughts that I placed binding restrictions on myself. I had not yet reached the realization that one's personal limitations are mainly the product of one's own mind. I had not recognized the simple fact that I had as much potential, as much right to be accepted as anyone else; that I could not only cope with life but find it enjoyable."

Pam struggled to get a master's degree while maintaining a home and family. Her husband and family were against her ambitions; no one, not even Pam, attended her graduation: "My optimism turned to a deep, black depression like none I'd ever experienced before. I climbed into bed and didn't get out for five years.

"I had finally reached bottom....I did not wish to live another day in such an atmosphere....Neither, I decided, did I want to take my own life.... That decision left me with only one course of action: I was going to have to do something to set my own house in order....I made up my mind that I was going to find a better way of living...if it killed me."

Pam didn't die. She decided to take control of her own life. During the unproductive years of her marriage she had gained considerable weight. She began by getting herself physically in shape. With the encouragement of her workout trainer she studied the tapes of Zig Ziglar, the motivational speaker. She then started selling advertising for the health club she belonged to.

From there she moved on to selling ads for radio and ended up working for Shamrock Broadcasting. Pam became vicepresident of Shamrock within two and a half years of beginning work with them. She was told—too late, fortunately—that this was impossible! "One of the most exciting things about ambition is that, once in full stride, it knows no bounds. No sooner is one goal reached than another is set. Motivation begins to feed on itself; momentum creates more momentum."

Pam Lontos did not succeed on her charm. She succeeded through hard work, the ability to learn quickly, and her ability to increase sales figures dramatically. The charm came later.

Pam worked her way up from an abyss. She made her decision to live, found something she loved to do, focused her efforts in that direction and then chose to act. She made the Decision to live her life fully and follow her dream. She acknowledged no blocks, she set her course and created her own new life filled with joy and success.

A useful exercise is to choose your heroes and read about their lives. You may admire Mother Teresa, who gave up a life of wealth and went against the preferences of her family, her order, the authorities in India, and anyone else she had to, in order to do her life's work. Or Lee Iacocca, who took on the automotive industry and did it "his way." Or

---

Everyone has a message, his life is his message.

Mohandas K. Gandhi

Liza Minnelli, who was brave enough to walk in her mother's footsteps and yet make her own way.

The Purpose of reading biographies of famous people is *not to emulate what they did, but to learn how they did it.* There are very few "overnight" successes. Each of our heroes has made the decision to live their Purpose and their Passion. Pavarotti has said that he had a very ordinary voice when he started singing with a boys' choir. But he had passion and drive. His voice is now magnificent! Successful people have internal direction. They tap into their inner courage. They are able to experience the thrill of meeting others' needs by meeting the powerful internal need of their own to be most truly who they are. The key is to *decide to do what you want to do and then do it!*

The Storeroom of Broken Dreams

Our storage room of "I can't," the room of broken tools, inadequate skills, and misgivings, is constantly entered and re-entered when we reinforce old ideas about the world being a hostile and negative place from which we need to be protected. We prove these fears to be true by believing in them, never dreaming that we have simply walked down the wrong hallway and opened the wrong door.

To enter the room of "I will" requires a decision to change our perception and change our direction. People who live their lives with Passion find the "I wills" become a new habit–and a habit just as strong as the "I can'ts." When you to through the doorway to "I will," you find all of the skills and talents and faith that you will ever need to be yourself.

It is easy to enter the right room. The more we practice entering the room that gives us strength and makes us feel good, the more energy we will have to live our Purpose and our Passion.

Exercise
Opening the Right Door

- Allow about 15 minutes for this exercise.
- Settle into a comfortable chair and let yourself relax.
- Breathe slowly and deeply, letting the relaxation deepen.
- As you relax, begin to clear your mind by picturing a white or yellow light. Allow the light to fill the spaces of your mind.
- As you continue to relax, begin to picture in your mind a long hallway in the clouds.
- On either side of the hallway you see a door. The door on the left says "The Door to Broken Dreams." In this room you will find all

your lists of inadequacies and can'ts. Push open the door and look inside.

How do you picture your "can'ts?" Your "can'ts" may look like shards of broken glass, or fallen leaves, or papers littering the floor, or bricks, or gooey, immobilizing blobs. Take a moment to open your eyes and in the space below draw your image of your "can'ts".

• Close your eyes now and return to the Room of Broken Dreams.

• Look around the room and say a final farewell. Leave the Room of Broken Dreams and close the door firmly behind you. You can lock and bolt it if you like...and throw away the key! You need never to return to this room again.

• Cross the hallway to the room with a sign on the door saying "The Door to Success." In this room you will find all your talents, your happy times, your strong desires for your life and your affirmations.

• Enter the Door to Success. What colors, sights, people and images do you see here? Notice the details of who and what is here. On the walls of this room in large golden letters are lists of your resources, talents, capabilities, personal characteristics, friends and helpers. Everyone in this room is admiring the wonderful things you have created and the wonderful person behind them.

• On one of the walls in this room you will see a writing board. On this board write down an affirmation statement about your Purpose and your Passion.

• Take your time. Have the patience to let your statement come through from your deepest self. If you want inspiration, all you have to do is glance at the wonderful things written on the walls. When the thought of your affirmation forms, write your statement on the board. For example:

I am alive, awake, alert and enthusiastic.
I am successful, ambitious and content.
I am honest, straightforward and powerful.
I am doing what I love and loving what I do.

- Read your affirmation statement three times. As you read the statement, relax your shoulders, smooth your brow and put a smile on your face.
  - Leave the room and go back through the hallway in the clouds.
  - Slowly allow the picture to fade, and open your eyes.
  - Breathe deeply and comfortably.
  - Enjoy the sense of relaxation and personal empowerment.
  - Write your success affirmation in the space below.

_____

_____

_____

_____

Choosing the Right Door

What can keep you out of the room called "I will?" One of the most important things to realize is that we cannot go through the door of the room "I will" while we are still in the room called "I can't." Going from one to the other requires a return to your perceptual base, which we may think of as the hallway. We can perceive the universe in which we live to be good or bad, harmful or benevolent, giving or withholding. But in reality the universe is none of those things. *The universe simply is, and it is abundant.* The good, benevolent, giving universe is found in the room "I will"; the withholding, harmful, negative universe is found in the room "I can't."

It is your beliefs and attitudes that determine which room you enter. The universe appears to give or withhold on the basis of your perceptions, not on the basis of its own reality. Each time you say "I can't," "I wish I could," or "If only..." you reinforce being in the wrong room. Changing your perception of a world of limitation and impossibilities simply requires the decision to do so. Once the decision is made, the rest is easy. We then act on the decision.

You can't solve a problem using the same kind of thinking that got you into the problem in the first place.

Albert Einstein

That Sounds Easy; Is It Really?

The leap of faith called decision can happen in an instant. It requires a simple change in thinking. Although this change is simple, it is not necessarily easy. To understand that we should stop a bad habit is simple, but stopping the habit is not always easy! To intellectually understand that smoking or overeating may be hazardous to our health may be simple, while changing the habit may not be. What is essential is that you decide to make the change. Once you put conviction behind a change in your habits, the process becomes easier and easier.

By changing our thoughts we can change our lives. Dr. Albert Ellis, the father of Rational-Emotive therapy says, "If you will change the way you act, you must change the way you think." He works as a therapist to help people take conscious control of their thoughts, feelings, and emotions. He helps them to understand why they think as they do, and to replace inappropriate behavior by first changing inappropriate thinking. *Our thoughts, led by our perceptions, over time become our beliefs. Our beliefs determine our behavior, our behavior then determines the consequences, and the consequences validate our perceptions.* This becomes a vicious circle spiraling steadily downward IF AND ONLY IF you do not intervene in order to determine your thoughts. If you do, you change the whole cycle, at its source, to a positive, life-affirming adventure in consciousness.

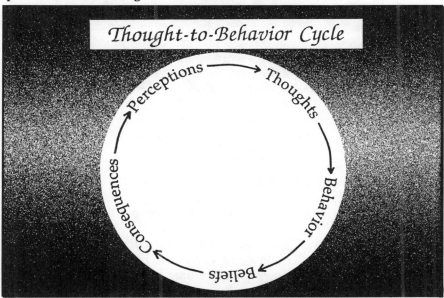

Thought-to-Behavior Cycle

Perceptions → Thoughts → Behavior → Beliefs → Consequences → Perceptions

Investigate your self-talk around decision-making. How do you talk yourself out of action? Do you find "I can't" or "It'll never work" separating your Purpose from your living?

My friend Tony deals with his negative self-talk first by recognizing when he is into it. Then he asks, "Is this real?" He says that 97% of the time it is not true. He then asks what the payoff is for thinking negative thoughts–usually it allows him to avoid risk. He can immobilize himself. When things are going well he uses his negative thoughts to help him self-correct to his old, poor self-image. In other words, his negative self-talk can take him home to the old comfortable place of "I can't." His new positive self-talk requires that he exercise change in his life. There is always a payoff for negative thinking as well as positive thinking; it is our choice which way we go.

Let's take a look at decision-making self-talk.

Exercise
Self-Talk and Decision-Making

- Take about 10 minutes for this exercise.
- Go to a quiet place that assures privacy.
- Allow yourself to get comfortable and relax.
- Relax all of your muscles and breathe slowly and deeply.
- Close your eyes and relax your mind.
- Go to your special favorite place.
- Think about the decision you want to make about your new direction, your Passion. Write it down below, or in your journal.
- Take note of any negative thinking that creeps into your mind.
- What kinds of limitations are you putting on yourself?
- Open your eyes and record the negative statements.
- Using the skills you have already learned, neutralize those statements by releasing the false ones and finding solutions for the ones that may have some truth to them. Write down your responses in your journal, or below.

Examples:
I feel the strength of my Decision to act on my Passion deep within my being.

I want to write and communicate with people in this wonderful way.

I know I can be a great singer/secretary/gardener, and from this moment, every step will be an expression of this Purpose.

I will let none of my own programming stand in the way of being fully myself.

I deeply commit myself to fulfilling my potential.

I feel the shift of personal power in my body as I KNOW that I will fulfill my Purpose.

I make a decision to move toward my Passion in the following way:

_____

_____

_____

Negative thoughts and limitations:

Example:

I don't have enough money to start this project.

It won't hurt to put off a decision a little bit longer.

I am not good enough/skilled enough/brave enough to do this project/job switch/artwork.

I've never done anything like this before.

What will happen if I try–and fail?

Nobody in my family ever did anything like this before.

I'll lose all the security I've built up if I change.

Your limitations:

_____

_____

_____

_____

_____

Positive options that support your decision:

Self-Embracing Statements:

What are some ways that I might obtain the money to start this project?

I know I've always been supported in my growth in the past. It will happen again.

I am a person who follows my dreams with action.

The universe is benevolent and I am its child.

Who can teach me what I need?

I do have the skills that I need. I affirm my own power and capabilities.

I can grow beyond my boundaries. I am ready to do this again.

I am not seeking to please others; I am seeking to fulfill my own potential.

Your Self-Embracing Statements:

_____

_____

_____

_____

_____

As we have already learned, our thoughts can create a neat little package of self-fulfilling prophecy and negative thinking–or they can create a world of learning, joy and interest. Negative thinking creates the appearance of negative and limited existence; positive thinking lets in the fresh air of change and opportunity. Change your thoughts and change your life. At any time of the day when you find yourself in the room of "I can't," return to the hallway (your perceptual base) and take yourself to the room of "I can."

When you hear the familiar "yes, but..." send it back where it belongs, to the room of "I can"t. It's just like a little animal that has escaped. We can pack it off to where it belongs; we don't have to stop what we are doing and conform to its whims. We can live in joy, and all it takes is discipline, commitment, and desire. We can all be Pathwalkers, people who say "I will," ordinary people who choose to live extraordinary lives by being true to themselves.

Like It or Not, You're Always in Control!

The decision to act rightly, to live our Passion, is vital. Many of us live lives of quiet desperation, hurtful, unaware, thoughtless, mindless. We go through the motions day by day, subduing our feelings, experiencing conflicting thoughts, suppressing our real selves.

Here is a simple test of whether or not you are living your Passion: What do you feel as you get out of bed in the morning, as you drive to work, as you walk through the door of your office, store, plant, or construction site? Do you find yourself saying, "This is wonderful!

Another day of doing what I love. I feel great! I love it! This is truly my Passion. I would risk all for this! I feel alive, renewed and energized!"

You just might not feel this way. You may be saying, "I don't even want to get up." You may think, "I hate this. I'd give anything to be somewhere else. I feel trapped, hopeless. Why do I keep doing this day after day?"

If you are not saying "I love myself and what I do; I take great pride in my work," why not change? If you continue to live each day of each year in a state of thoughtless acceptance of the way things are, you will simply get one year older rather than one year better. If you choose to live your Purpose and your Passion, you will be joyfully alive, wiser and happier in ways that you might only dimly imagine now. The payoff for risk-taking and living fully is a life that is more intense, more brightly colored, more inwardly content and more meaningful.

Irene Falk is a person who is living her Passion for freedom and being with people. I met Irene when we were doing corporate training together for a large retail company. While having dinner the evening before the training program I discovered that Irene literally lived out of a suitcase. Now, being on the road is not my favorite thing and definitely not my Passion. And yet, here was a person who lived her life exactly as she chose, and she chose to live on the road. Here's how she tells her story:

"Where do I live? In a suitcase! I have no residence; my home is right here...wherever I am at the moment. I have no possessions other than those that fit into a small airline suitcase that fits under the seat. It holds two suits, one black skirt, eight blouses, two weeks' worth of underwear, one cardigan sweater, one vest, one turtleneck, two pairs of heels, one pair of boots and one pair of slacks. I have two necklaces, one pair of earrings, one watch. I also carry one coat in winter. If I need casual or dressy clothes for the weekend, I buy cheap ones and then leave them behind. I have been living in my suitcase for almost a year now. The biggest surprise was to learn how concerned people are about my lack of a home. I had never considered others' reactions.

"I live on the road and I love it. I have clean sheets every night and I throw the dirty towels on the floor. If I'm hungry I just pick up the phone and call room service. I've been referred to as a 'classy bag lady'– a fellow passenger in a limo called me a professional house guest because my weekends are usually spent with friends.

"How did this all come about? How did I end up with this kind of freedom in my 50s?

"I was widowed at age 41. My husband was only 42 and he died very suddenly. Up until that time I had been a good corporate wife and followed my husband all over the country as he moved up the corporate ladder. I learned how to pack, how to buy a house, how to sell a house and how to make new friends.

"I began to work as a product specialist for a large retail corporation. At that time I owned a beautiful home on five acres of land that took two people and three hours to mow. I owned horses and all of the responsibility that goes along with them. I had a lot of material possessions collected over a lifetime of family growth. After a week in Boston or New York, or wherever I was working, the house was a great place to come home to–that is, when I came home. I had already developed the habit of staying with friends in different cities, or going to professional conferences or events. My daughter loved the house and was thrilled to act as caretaker. But then she moved to Denver! Without her the house suddenly became a burden. It meant that I had to go home every weekend and take care of things. My house owned me!

"The question was, what to do with thirty years of household goods? I had moved 16 times in 21 years and I was not going to move this stuff again. Answer: I gave it all away to my children. I gave Monica blue stickers and Brian red stickers and said, 'Go through the house and tag what you want.' I called the movers and sent one truck to Monica in Denver and one truck to Brian in Dallas. Everyone who helped me pack up the rest was encouraged to take a pickup truck's worth home.

"I was left with a briefcase full of personal papers and one suitcase of personal clothes. What a surprise to realize, as I drove out of the gravel driveway in my rental car, that my tension had loosened and released. I felt myself smile. I stopped by a friend's house, and she commented on how happy I looked. I felt free–FREE! No husband, no kids, no animals, no house, no car, no responsibility for anyone but me. I had been afraid that I might feel lost, but I was found!

"Next came the task of figuring out how to work and live within this society without a permanent residence. Because I was traveling for my company during the week, they took care of all travel and hotel expenses. My frequent flyer awards covered most weekend hotels and car rentals. I arranged for a mailbox service to forward my mail each week. Banking is done with automatic deposits from my employer. Withdrawals are done with credit cards at airports and shopping centers. A financial advisor takes care of all taxes and statements, and I make phone calls with an AT&T calling card

"It all started with a job that had me traveling 100% of the time. I fell in love with the lifestyle and just added the weekends. In the last six months I've been to London and Scotland. I saw fall in Virginia and spent Christmas in Denver. Still, after I tell people this story, they often ask, 'Yes, but where do you really live?' "

Irene Falk has been willing to buck the tide and create a lifestyle that is uniquely hers. She broke out of the bounds of her past history and discovered her Passion despite the fact that she'd lived in the same house from kindergarten to college. She found out what she needed to do to live the way she wanted to. Once the decision was made, she went for it. She gave herself freedom.

How we behave right now is determined by how we have been practicing to be. Our behaviors are not predetermined. They are shaped and nurtured. It is important that we decide how we want to behave and then put all of our energy toward our goals. If we want to be decisive, then we need to practice making decisions. If we want to be strong we need to practice using our inner strength. The nonagenarian comedian George Burns, whose energy is legendary, was once asked why he doesn't seem to age with his contemporaries. He replied: "People get old because they *practice* being old. They start using their arms to heave them out of the chair rather than jumping out. They practice saying, 'I can't do that anymore, I'm too old.' Eventually, with enough practice, they achieve being old. I've never got into practice."

If we are shy or outgoing, it is primarily because we see ourselves that way. We then practice that view of ourselves. We set up an expectation in ourselves and others. A friend of mine once said, "I hate being the life of the party all of the time." It was interesting to note that others had said of her, "Sheila always seems to be the life of the party. That must be exhausting. I'll bet she'd like to slow down sometimes." When you catch yourself saying, "That's just the way I am," or "That's the way people expect me to be," change those statements to "That is the way I have been acting, but I have the power to change my behavior." Like it or not, you are always in control of your life, even when you choose to give that control to others.

Anything we have learned, we can change! If we mentally review the events of our lives, we will remember that if something caused us pain we changed it. And if we chose not to change the situation and continued to be in pain, that was also our choice. I was a marriage counselor for a long time. When people came in with their stories of painful relationships, they gave many reasons why they had stayed married. Yet it was interesting to note that those who came in to talk

---

New Hampshire Farmer: *Can I borrow your rope, neighbor?*
Neighbor: *Nope.*
Farmer: *And just why is that?*
Neighbor: *I'm using it to tie down my milk bucket.*
Farmer: *But you don't need a rope to tie down a milk bucket!*
Neighbor: *When you don't want to do something,*
one excuse is as good as another.

about why they were leaving often offered *exactly the same reasons.*
We make a decision–and then we fill in the details.

Take a moment to remember a time when you had to make a painful
decision.

Exercise
Handling Pain

- Close your eyes for a moment.
- Think about a painful change in your life.
- How did you feel when you realized that you had to make the
change?
- How did you feel after the change was made?
- How do you feel about the situation now?

Often when we think back we realize that much of our pain came
from indecision. The change or choice was difficult, but often we made
it more difficult for ourselves and others because we wanted to avoid
the responsibility of the decision.

Any marriage counselor can relate stories of people who will do
things to precipitate a change in the other person in order to force him
or her to make the decision. For example, many times people want to
get out of a relationship and may not really know why. The real issue is
often not that a third person is involved, but that something is amiss in
the relationship of the two people. Perhaps if it were identified it
could be worked out, and maybe not. What often happens is that in the
pain of indecision, one person will have an affair in order to precipitate
a crisis and cause the other person to react. With so much hurt the
relationship is doomed–and the real problem gets shoved under the rug.
This provides the opportunity to repeat the mistake with the next
person.

One couple who came to me for marriage counseling stands out in my
memory. They stated that they wanted to save their marriage. There
were hidden agendas, however. One was "take my side against my
partner." Another was "help me get out of this without experiencing
any guilt or pain." Another was "help me make my spouse wrong." The
most deeply hidden one was "help me grow up and take responsibility
for my life."

When they came to see me they were already separated. He had
an affair before they separated and now she was dating also. They felt
that they "should" work on getting back together again. The affair
had precipitated the crisis, but in truth, it was poor communication
that had destroyed the original trust, caring and joy in the relation-

ship. They wanted change in their lives, but they didn't know how to go about getting it.

One particular week, the woman could not keep the appointment, and I saw the man alone. One of the reasons he gave for their separation was that they shared nothing in common. As an example he mentioned that he loved to go camping but she didn't.

The following week, he couldn't come, so I saw the woman alone. She happened to tell me that she had been on a camping trip the week before and really loved it!

When the three of us met again, I asked the wife to tell her husband where she had been the prior week. She informed him that she had been camping. As I saw no reaction from him, I asked him how he felt about what his wife had just said. He answered that he hadn't really heard her. I asked her to repeat what she had said. He was shocked for a moment and then angry. He said that it was impossible that she could have been camping, since she hated camping. She shot back that she loved camping but that he had never wanted to take her on his trips. He started yelling that she never wanted to go. She yelled back that he never asked her!

These people had been married and living together for six years. Yet each had very little idea about who the other person was. They lived parallel lives, but did not communicate. When it came down to taking action to improve or terminate their relationship, neither was willing to make a decision. They were, however, still precipitating events while seeming to let the divorce "just happen." Marriage counselors hear this phrase often: "The divorce just happened," or "I don't know how, but we just sort of drifted apart."

This couple was not unusual. They had started out loving each other. Over the years they forgot to talk. They forgot what it was like to share ideas, dreams and desires. Neither wanted to hurt the other person, so they shared their ideas with other friends. They grew apart, felt guilty, avoided the decision to confront their problems, and the rest "just happened."

Maturity, inner courage, being an adult, has to do with being willing to take responsibility for your life. It means making the difficult decisions as well as the easy ones. It means standing up for what you believe and taking the consequences. It means being a real person and not the shadow of what you could be.

If wishes were horses, beggars would ride.

Old English Saying

If you have ever watched a soap opera you know that there could be no soap operas if people in the stories told the truth to each other. To have a successful soap opera requires that people "protect each other from the truth." They won't tell each other things because "they'll hate me." They must act irresponsibly and then blame others. They must avoid decisions at all costs. They must either be thoughtlessly selfish or completely selfless, with absolutely no regard for their own needs.

When real people make soap opera of their lives, they are stuck with the consequences *just as assuredly as they would be if they took total responsibility.* Our lives change for the better when we choose to act honestly and in good faith. When we are excited and growing, we acknowledge and accept our actions.

The opportunity is there at every moment of our lives to accept responsibility for our own self-management—or we can continue to pretend that we are "out of control" and not responsible. Why wait? We can begin now to take charge of our lives and make the decision to experience life to the fullest. We can choose power, joy, aliveness and excitement. Remember how you felt diving off of the high diving board. Imagine how it feels to sky-dive or remember what it was like when as a kid you rode the roller coaster. There you were at the crest of the first great drop. Just as the cars peaked at the top of the hill, you looked down at that huge chasm, the cars rolled slowly forward and you were suddenly thrust backward in your seat as the force of energy drove the cars forward. What exhilaration! We can experience that kind of exhilaration every single day of our lives.

Taking Responsibility for Our Choices

It is essential that we choose to accept personal responsibility for our choices. Every time we accept 100% responsibility for our lives, we change the world. The world changes because when we do take responsibility for our own lives we don't have to blame anybody else. When we don't have to blame anybody else, we don't have to be angry. When we are no longer angry we can put all of that energy into making the world a better place to live. And so, we can change the world. We can say, with Thea Alexander, that the little bit of the world that is me is working perfectly.

The price of greatness is responsibility.

Winston Churchill

Wishing is a waste of our time and energy and wishing does *not* make it so. Choice makes it so; making a decision and acting on it with one hundred percent intention. When we fall into wishing, we sap our energy, give credence to our excuses, and waste our lives. *We really do know what we want; we simply need to accept it.*

All too often we refuse to follow our dream, that inner message, because it seems as if it couldn't possibly support us. How about chocolate chip cookies? It worked for Mrs. Fields and Wally "Famous" Amos. Forget about "shoulds" and "if onlys" and "it'll never pay." Do your part in the whole of life and the whole of life will support you. Doing your part requires one hundred percent commitment, dedication and focus.

Where to Start?

If you approach change one step at a time, you will slowly remove limitations and fears. Life changes actually occur in an instant, yet at the same time, they are cumulative. Since we can never be certain when that transforming moment will be, we need to move consistently toward our goal.

Understanding that we are all Pathwalkers is the first step. Accepting our Path and loving the journey are the next steps. Truly living life is the ultimate goal.

Knowing your Passion, what you love to do, gives you direction. The advantage of knowing your Purpose and living your Passion is that you can use each new piece of information you discover to learn and grow and change. We redirect, learn, build, and alter because we have a blueprint for our lives, not a job description. It is the Path that is critical, not the daily "how to's." Any good leader will give others an objective to reach, and then allow them the opportunity to accomplish the task through their own individual creativity, not specifying how it will be done. Be a good leader to yourself, letting your life unfold as your learn more and more about who you are and the direction you are moving in.

Once you have made your decision to act, you can develop an action plan for how you will move, putting one foot in front of the other to

---

Life is like a tapestry that we see from below:
We see only the thread we are weaving right now;
God sees the whole pattern from above.

Corrie Ten Boom

make orderly progress. If your progress toward your goal requires certain steps, plan them and take them one day at a time. If you want to climb mountains, first take a basic mountain-climbing course. Move on to short trips and then to more serious events. You'll always be able to get there one step at a time. Make your decision and all else will follow.

Mike Speakman attended my Pathwalkers course in 1987. Mike was in the process of change. He had already been very successful in his life. From 1963 to 1970 he worked for a Fortune 100 company as an engineer. He became restless and left, to the dismay of the company. He was told that there would always be a place for him, but Mike sought challenge and change.

From 1970 to 1979 Mike was a successful real estate agent and made enough money to sell his business in 1979 and retire. He began to search again for new horizons.

Mike always felt that he had a certain Purpose. He saw his Purpose as being a bridge for people. In his work as an engineer, Mike saw his strength as helping the engineers and technicians communicate and get along. The part of real estate that he liked best was conducting the negotiations. He felt that he could help people come to a happier conclusion with better communication. Mike enjoys bridging the gaps between people and helping them to enjoy their lives more.

In 1980, Mike began another career, in personal counseling. He opened the Listening Center, which was aimed at helping people communicate better in business and in their personal lives. He counseled many people in the area of personal growth and change.

At one time he ran a class called Discover Your Passion. Other courses were in the areas of active listening, making successful presentations, and stress management. Mike felt that he was the bridge for people between where they were in their lives and where they wanted to be.

Then Mike decided that he wanted to switch to a counseling job helping people bridge the gap between their addictions and their strengths. He wanted to help people find the inner strength to let go of their addictions. He wished to encourage them to make their own personal decision to act from the best of who they really are. He had previously worked as a volunteer counselor with the Crisis Hotline, the Rape Crisis Center, the V.A. Hospital and his own programs.

One of the exercises in my Pathwalkers seminar includes getting help from the person sitting next to you. This person becomes your "spiritual partner," a friend who agrees to help or advise you whenever possible.

Mike's block was that he feared that someone without a college degree would not be able to get a job as a professional clinical counselor. Mike's partner was a woman who worked with the Salvation Army.

They took the seminar together and vowed to help each other whenever they could.

After the seminar, Mike called his partner, who worked as the clinical director for the Salvation Army, and found that the organization was looking for a counselor for its addiction program. Mike was hired based on the skills and background he obtained in the nineteen years of training that he offered and received. He was hired even though he doesn't have a college degree. At the Salvation Army, Mike is working to help people with addictions bridge the gap to their strengths.

Mike challenged his limitations; he confronted his fears and made the decision to go after what he wanted in life in order to live his Purpose. He took the risk, and was supported.

Support Follows Decision

Another thing that Mike did was to access his strengths. One of those strengths was his spiritual partner from the Pathwalkers course. Accepting help from our friends and acquaintances is certainly not a new idea. It has been suggested by many, the most formidable being Napoleon Hill in his book *Think and Grow Rich.* Hill suggested a principle called "Master Minding." A Master Mind group is a group of people dedicated to one cause. They are in agreement as to outcomes and open to process. Members of the group agree to help each other to accomplish a particular outcome. The process of Master Minding has been used to help people and teams reach a specified goal.

A Master Mind group can be large or small; it can even be just one other person. It can be a formal group with regular meetings and guidelines or it can be made up of old friends who help each other. The important aspect of Master Minding is the willingness to help each other and the willingness to have fun while doing it. The process includes brainstorming–letting ideas flow without censure. Sometimes the craziest ideas lead to the most satisfactory outcomes.

Master Mind groups are resource groups for both tangible and intangible resources. One person may need some help with a new computer and can offer tennis lessons in return. Often the greatest resource the group can offer is unconditional support. There are so many people willing to tell us why we can't do something, it is pure pleasure to have people who will help us find out how we can!

Several years ago, I decided to go to Japan to teach, travel and study Japanese business practices. I also wanted to break from my normal routine and have an opportunity to gain some perspective on my life. I began to brainstorm with my Master Mind group. I discovered that one friend had already lived in Japan and she was able to give me job leads. One of her acquaintances then led me to a job. I began taking

Japanese language lessons at night school and interviewed people in the international business community for information and guidance.

I contacted friends in Hawaii and ended up staying there for three months on my way to Japan. I wanted to learn more about the Pacific Rim business community, and so I attended workshops at the University of Hawaii and the East West Center. It seemed as though every person I met gave me new ideas and suggested future options. Each one either knew someone, or knew someone who knew someone, who would be helpful. One by one, I found answers to all my needs. I found a place to stay, a place to teach, and many friends and business contacts. I had a much fuller experience because I was willing to receive help and guidance from others.

Master Mind groups use the process of networking or interaction to benefit each member of the group in different ways. We will not always be able to repay people on a one-to-one basis and that is not really necessary. What is required is that we help when we can. The first rule for a successful Master Mind group is the willingness of each member to help whenever they are able. The second is to have fun doing it. The third rule is to be fair; this means that everyone in the group gets help from the others when they need it.

The Master Mind group is just one way of helping ourselves to achieve our goals. The major step, however, is making the decision.

The time for you to begin acting on your dreams is *now*. Every moment you spend in the wrong room of "I can't" whittles away at your existence. At this very moment you can make the decision to live your life!

All that has come before is the preparation for this chapter. This is the great event of your life. I am often asked, "All of this is fine and well, but how do I actually change?" The answer is always and forever the same: you must *decide*. The decision is everything. Without the decision to act, you have nothing more than one more interesting intellectual exercise. You have the choice of deciding for your life and your Purpose, or choosing to live without soul and without Passion.

On page 184 you will find a contract of agreement to begin to live your Purpose and Passion consciously. Do not enter upon this contract lightly. It is a contract of the heart. Enter into it only with a committed

---

Some people make things happen.
Some people watch things happen.
Some people ask, "What happened?"

Anonymous

spirit, with a heart full of joy and wonder. There is no shame in delaying this decision, for that also is your decision. Each Path you choose to take *must be your own unique Path,* your truth. Each lesson is your lesson. Each turn in the road is your turn.

If the decision to act on your Purpose seems difficult, remember those times when you finally got sick and tired of the way things were. You decided then and there that you would change–and you did! That is what decision is. Decisions do not take a long time or a lot of analysis. The decisions for right action are always in the background of our mind and spirit.

Exercise
The Right Decision

- Before you turn the page, take a moment to be alone with yourself.
- Close your eyes and allow your mind and body to relax.
- With your eyes gently closed, look deep inside yourself for the inner strength to make the right choice.
- Ask yourself the question, "Am I truly willing to commit myself to my own growth?"
- Look for any self-doubts, any restrictions, and mentally write them down on a piece of paper. Place them in an envelope.
- Walk to the door to the room of broken dreams and slip the envelope through the mail slot in the door.
- Relax again.
- With a full heart, choose to commit to your own best life.
- Open your eyes and fold your hands to remind yourself of your inner strength.
- When you are ready and relaxed, fill out and sign the contract with yourself.

The Decision Contract

Right now you have the opportunity to commit to yourself and your own great Purpose and Passion by making a binding agreement with yourself. On the next page is a contract for you to fill out, date and sign. You may choose to keep it in the book or to cut it out and put it in a prominent place. This contract is for you only. It is your promise to yourself to live your life fully.

Personal Contract

I _____,
hereby commit to living my Purpose always. I choose to
live a life consistent with my belief in myself and in
my life's greater meaning. I choose to accept
one hundred percent responsibility for my life.
I accept a vision of living my life fully,
as a powerful, able, happy being.
I agree to live my Passion as long as it serves my Purpose.
I am willing to let go of my Passion
when it no longer serves my Purpose.
I commit to always taking time to identify
my next step along the Path.

Signed _____ Date _____

Affirmations
The Decision

Your decision can be summed up in one concise statement that embodies the full strength of your intention. Take a moment now to formulate and refine a statement that embodies the essence of your decision. Make it snappy and memorable, so that it will be easily available to you during those times when your decision seems dim and distant. Some examples of effective decision affirmations are:

Thank God, I'm being myself at last!
I know who I am, I know the power of who I am, and nothing can shake me.
There is nothing more important than my Purpose.
I give myself the gift of all of myself.
I know that I am a valuable human being.

Your Decision Affirmation:

_____

_____

_____

To strengthen and reinforce this commitment contract, each day when you awake, and before you arise to start your day's activities, take a moment to let your mind soar with your decision affirmation. Do the same thing in the evening before you fall asleep. Remind yourself of what your greater Purpose in life is and the way you are now choosing to manifest this Purpose through your Passion.

Our Purpose has no power without the decision or commitment to act. Acting on our decision is the demonstration of our belief in ourselves.

Everyone has a message:
His life is his message.

Mohandas Gandhi

Pathwalker: Dr. Charles Garfield

Dr. Charles Garfield is the author of *Peak Performers, The New Heroes of American Business*, a well-known researcher and speaker on peak performance and the founder of the Shanti Project in San Francisco, California. The Shanti Project is a professional counseling service to aid dying patients and their families. The word *Shanti* is a Hindu word meaning "peace that passeth all understanding."

From NASA to Shanti

"The concept of the Shanti Project emerged from a fascinating work situation," Dr. Garfield explains. "In 1967, I started my career as a mathematician on Apollo 11, the first moon landing. It was there that I first saw people doing unexpectedly superior work. Wherever I turned, some man or woman, some group or team was producing at levels far beyond anything they had done before. I became curious about how and why such peak performance happens, how people are inspired to accomplish their best work. I decided that my mission was to find out what peak performance was all about.

"Neil Armstrong took that 'one small step for a man' and shortly thereafter my beloved Apollo team fell apart. Some of our best people left because there were no further challenges. After waiting around for a mission worth sinking our teeth into, a mission that compelled us to make a contribution, many people simply gave up. We were working in a large bureaucratic organization, which, during the Apollo project, housed some of the most inspired people I have ever seen. But afterward, with no mission, the spirit was gone. I wanted to find out what had really happened on Apollo 11, why we did such superior work. So I returned to school and received a Ph.D. in clinical psychology from U.C. Berkeley, and formally committed myself to a life's mission centering on the study of peak performances. My main interest became those people who make great impact and sustained contributions over the long haul."

The Psychology of Survivors

"One of the first research projects I became involved in was the study of cancer survivors, a group of people who seemed to me to be high achievers," Dr. Garfield says "Almost every one of them was dealing with the issue of personal survival. The characteristics shared by these cancer survivors did indeed resemble those of the high achievers I remember on the Apollo 11 and in fact matched the high achievers I have known well in the Shanti Project, business, the professions, sports, and the arts. These are the characteristics I found were common to all high achievers:

I. They had a clear sense of mission.

These folks were motivated by a powerful sense of personal mission, a mission that was a healthy one, that allowed them to grow and contribute. Such missions constitute the best of motivations and we have certainly found them among people who commit to Shanti.

II. The second characteristic is "results in real time."

They not only had an over-arching mission but were specifically goal-oriented, results-oriented. Many people confuse mission and goals. Mission is a statement of your basic commitment, goals are the measurable steps toward completing that mission. Simply put, goals are dreams with deadlines.

III. The third is self-management through self-mastery.

These were people who took initiative, people who managed themselves well because they knew themselves well. They knew their strengths and those areas that needed improvement. They saw themselves as human resources to be perfected, to grow, possessing vast human potential.

IV. Team-building and team-playing.

I found that the peak performers I studied were not Lone Ranger types; they were collaborators. They knew, as did our Shanti clients, that nobody survives without help. We have certainly found the same thing to be true of Shanti volunteers over the years. Nobody does this work without assistance, emotional support, and, in fact, support of many kinds.

V. The fifth characteristic is course correction.

These were not people who never made a mistake, who never got lost in trying to achieve their mission. They were people who knew how to find their way back on track again.

VI. The last characteristic is the ability to manage change.

These are folks who realize that every once in a while the world throws you a curve ball; it can be change in the rules or change in the major elements of what you are doing. One major change was our shift in focus from cancer to AIDS. Had there not been something about the form of Shanti Project that allowed it to adapt quickly, it would have been history. There is something about the ability of these individuals to move with not just rapid change, but with radical change.

Life Influences Change

"I began doing the research on peak performance," Dr. Garfield says, "but the power of the work I was doing with the Shanti Project was so much greater that I had to reinterpret my mission. It may sound peculiar to say that something was more important than the first moon landing, given the magnitude of that project. I was thrust into a situation where I had to shift gears in a major way.

"Shanti is really about being the absolute best we can be in a situation demanding peak performance and compassion. So although I did not forget the main intent of my research, I extended the focus from cancer survivors to Shanti volunteers. Also from cancer survivors and peak performers in general, to health professionals working with seriously ill patients and families, grieving persons dealing with the loss of a loved one, and the dying men and women themselves.

"One of the first challenges was the search for a volunteer agency model that could help me with the work I was doing. I was already tremendously overloaded in my assignment at the Cancer Research Institute at the University Medical School in San Francisco. I was in charge of the psychological needs of a large oncology unit and was rapidly learning what many of us learn: that people don't care how much you know until they know how much you care. Often caring takes time and compassion and always takes emotional accessibility. From my point of view as the helper, I needed assistance in doing the work well. As the original Shanti volunteer, I had many clients who were in various stages of their disease, some dying and some dealing with the aftermath of chemotherapy, radiation therapy, and surgery.

"As anybody who does this work in a compassionate way quickly finds out, you get hooked not only by the emotional needs of the people you work with, but also by the importance of the work itself. I began to realize that I not only needed help but also became fascinated by what a community-based group of helpers could do to take care of a very real human issue. This was true whether the people we worked with survived or whether they died; compassionate caring and help made sense in either context.

"At the time there was far less sensitivity to the psychological, spiritual, and emotional needs of people facing a life-threatening illness. I spent days at the bedsides of very ill people, listening, learning, and helping as best I could. I listened to them carefully as they tried to help me understand what they were going through.

"I saw many health professionals doing their best to treat their patients for physical ailments while having little time, energy or skills necessary for dealing with the psychological and spiritual stresses and strains. My psychological skills were certainly useful at various points, but the single strongest asset I had, and the single strongest asset the Shanti volunteer has, is the willingness to walk into the emotional life of another person when invited to do so; to be there for people as fully and consciously as one can; to feel a little of what our clients feel; to share with them their hopes and dreams, and to be available in whatever way made sense. This is far less psychotherapy than it is human compassion.

"When we are available to other human beings, particularly in times of major stress, we have learned the very first lesson of the Shanti Project: To be emotionally accessible to people, patients and their friends and families, without carrying with us all sorts of extraneous agendas and frameworks and preconceived models about how helping and caring is supposed to take place or how spiritual and psychological support is supposed to take place, but rather to be really available as an advocate."

Transition

"One of the benefits and burdens of doing the work of the Shanti Project is that when you are perceived as helpful, you get asked to do more work," Dr Garfield continues. "In a fairly short period of time, it became obvious that there was too much for me to do alone, and that I clearly needed some help. It didn't have to be a professional organization at all. In fact, those best suited for this work were likely to be people who were willing to challenge their precious peace of mind, minimize the distance between themselves and those they worked with and go into a helping situation whether or not they had the so-called 'objectivity' so often associated with formalized psychotherapy. It occurred to me, that we could train carefully selected volunteers to do this work extremely well.

"I began to call family members of patients I had worked with, health professionals who I knew would do a good job, even patients who were in long-term remission, and simply asked the question, 'Would you be interested in joining a volunteer group committed specifically to the care of patients, their friends and family members, people who are seriously ill, and those who are grieving.' From the dozens of phone calls made I selected about twenty people to be the original Shanti volunteers and who would provide both the quality of care and the commitment necessary to launch the project.

"Our volunteers thought of themselves as folks who would listen, talk, be available. Their training came from the best of the counseling traditions but their willingness to give the best of themselves came from a deeper source. Originally, it never occurred to me that counseling was only for licensed counselors. It seemed that some of these 'professional skills' could be taught to lay individuals. We taught people how to listen. We taught them how to respond to a variety of questions they didn't have answers to....Some people left when they saw that they would not be able to face the challenge. I always saw leaving as a courageous act when someone knew that he or she would not be able to do the work.

"Our fledgling organization was really doing incredible work...in 1976, 1977, and 1978, major conferences were held at the University of California at San Francisco. I chaired these conferences which were called 'Care of the Dying Patient' and were directed at physicians and other health providers. These were major training conferences and Shanti Project took part in all of them....People came by the hundreds to devote three days to learn how to care for dying people and their families....and they were taught largely by our volunteers. Over 300 organizations had used the Shanti model by the end of the 1970s in the United States alone. In 1979 the National Center for Voluntary Action gave me their National Activist of the Year award, which I accepted on behalf of Shanti Project.

"By 1978 we had become a project with two separate functions: training and patient advocacy. The plan between 1978 and 1980 was to decrease the amount of direct service, because this was increasingly provided by other agencies, and to increase the amount of time and resources we committed to the training and referral functions. Our plan was for Shanti to become primarily an international training resource and information clearinghouse."

The Challenge

"With the emergence of the first AIDS referral in 1980, there began to be a challenge to our vision. By this I mean, here was a new and overwhelming problem which obviously needed to be addressed and, at the same time, Shanti had moved away from direct support toward the training, referral, and information clearinghouse model. We were faced with a choice: we could begin again to do what we had done historically to meet the needs of patients, friends and families--or hope that someone else would take care of it. That is where we were needed, and that is where we went.

"The call was put out for more people. We 'geared up' again, but in the new direction. What amazed so many of us, myself included, was that the Shanti model could be adapted so quickly to a major change in focus. We had developed a form or model that moved swiftly to meet the AIDS crisis.

Personal Transition—The Decision

"This was a time for major change for me as well. I had been doing the work nonstop for more than eight years. I had sat with more than 300 people who had died, mostly at the Cancer Institute and through the work of the Shanti Project. I had already moved to emphasize the training function and toward integrating my Shanti work with my original study of peak performance. I had seen in my own experience at Shanti, that when people remained too long they often became unable to realize it was time to go. They often created problems for themselves and others. I knew I needed to avoid this particular outcome for myself. The study of peak performance, my original life's mission, was calling and I knew that I had to respond. At this point, Shanti was in the hands of people who cared about it a great deal. I agreed to be available but made it very clear that I was going to step back.

"As I look back on this period, it is clear to me that I needed to move away from daily contact with the project in order to gain perspective. I had gone through a decade of tremendously arduous commitment and involvement. I needed some time and space to write about it and to allow myself to see it as part of my study of peak performance."

Charles Garfield knew when to make the decision to create something, when to stay with it, when to change and when to leave. Each decision is equally important and each one builds our lives.

Living Your Vision

Vision has power, strength, and clarity. It is the eternal link between awareness and our reality. When we are able to "see" our truth and our Purpose, we have a depth of knowing that is communicated inwardly and outwardly. Others observing us see the power of our Vision. People with a clear Vision cannot be swayed from their direction nor from the integrity of their behavior. Vision provides a source of comfort and strength when circumstances around us are discouraging. Vision is powerful in its ability to guide the course of external events.

Finding a Vision

How do we find a Vision that reflects the truth of our innermost being?

Our imagination is the key to change, the key to accepting the guidance of our higher selves. All that we envision already exists. Our task is to place ourselves in that picture consciously and with strong emotion. Everything we experience with deliberate intent and strong emotion is recorded in our lives forever, and becomes part of the record of who we are. Our Vision takes us from where we are today to the place where we want to be. Our dream today is our destiny tomorrow.

Imagination is more important than knowledge.

Albert Einstein

As we begin to unfold our desires in our dreams, the universe responds with gifts of accomplishment.

What if you think that you don't have a good imagination? It is true that some people seem to be able to envision or see pictures more easily than others. For some it will come naturally, for others, with practice. There will also be people who will *hear* their pictures rather than see them. Others will *feel* their pictures. When I relax and visualize, I sometimes see "real" pictures, but just as frequently I will "feel" a picture or an answer. It will just come to me and I will know that I know. The important thing is to utilize whichever sense modality works best for you. When you ask yourself how you know when something is right, you will get a sense of what sense modality you work from: sight, sound, smell or touch.

The next exercise will help you discover how you visualize.

Exercise
The Source of Imagination

- Allow about 10 minutes for this exercise.
- Relax your body and your mind.
- Clear your mind by picturing the color yellow or a bright white light.
- Call to mind something you really like. For me, it's sunset on the desert.
- As you call this event or scene to mind, pay attention to how you experience it. Do you see it, hear it, smell it, feel it or all of the above? For example, when I "picture" a sunset on the desert I see the purple, rose and blue colors of the sky. I see the incredible beauty of the mountains, the sand and the cactus. But mostly I "feel" the heat of the sand and the air, I feel the peace of the surroundings, I feel the vibrant life of the desert. My strongest sense modality is the sense of touch.
- Note which sense modality you used this time.

You won't always access the same sense modality. It takes practice to identify which sense you are using at any moment. One is not better than another. Each is simply one means of access to experience. We all have the ability to visualize in one way or another. The important thing is to take control of this capability and actively employ it to benefit your life. We use Vision to move toward our future with greater ease.

Throughout the ages, our greatest thinkers and doers have reveled in their imaginations. They have acknowledged this power within and allowed it to reveal to them the information, pictures, ideas and secrets of the universe.

We all have access to this power, and this pool of information is available to us all. Einstein said that all of the knowledge of the universe is available to us if we just listen. Edison, Ford, Napoleon Hill, Socrates and other great thinkers and scientists have acknowledged that their greatness came from their ability to pull from this universal knowledge to which we all have access. They knew that they sometimes needed to be still and listen, to acknowledge what they already knew.

Sometimes we receive information by testing and testing, testing, and testing again, until the clouds of our own wants and expectations clear and our Path is made known to us. Alexander Graham Bell is an example of courage and strength and tenacity. Bell not only worked tirelessly on his inventions, but he fought to maintain his rights as well. Bell stood by his inventions and by his own integrity. Inventors, creators and artists are people whom we admire because they are dedicated to their work. They succeed because they don't give up. Small business failures are quite often the result of someone giving up when the going gets rough. Those who succeed are those who hold their Vision and keep going because they love what they are doing and they believe that they can succeed.

Our Vision carries us into the future which already exists if we simply become enraptured with it. We need to always accept our Vision and fill it with Passion. We cannot be passive about our Purpose. If we are, we lose it. Give your Passion all the life you have and it will return that life to you a hundredfold. As we begin to revel in our dreams, to unfold our destiny, the universe responds with all that we will ever need to live our Purpose.

You have identified your Purpose and your Passion. Let's take a moment to visualize living that Passion.

The first time you did this exercise it was a beginning. Since that time you have identified your resources and your strengths. You have released your blocks and inhibitions. This time you will be able to envision living your Passion without restraint.

Imagination rules the world.

Napoleon Bonaparte

Exercise
Imagining Unrestrained Passion

- Allow about 10 minutes for this exercise.
- Find a comfortable chair and let yourself relax totally.
- Clear your mind by picturing the color yellow or a bright white light.
- Begin to visualize yourself living your Passion. What are you doing? How are you dressed? What do you look like? What colors do you see in this Vision of your Passion. What people are present? What can you smell, touch, taste? Picture as many details of this scene as possible.
- Enjoy the Vision. Revel in it. Embrace it.
- Allow your thoughts to come back into the room.
- Remember the feeling of living your Passion. It is yours and only yours.

Each time you visualize the good in your life, your dreams, you give them power. You create your life by what you hold in your mind. Hold your dreams dearly in your heart. No one else will love them more than you do.

The courage of our Vision comes from the decision that we have made regarding our Purpose. Vision itself offers us unlimited freedom. It puts life in our wishes and excitement in our dreams. Vision is one of the greatest unblockers that we have available to us. When we are willing to take the time to call on our imagination, to tap into the universe, to let go of our limitations and expectations and to open ourselves to the infinite storehouse of possibility, the universe rewards us.

Unlimited Vision

It is important that we do not set limits on our Vision. When we receive our Vision we must accept it in its wholeness. We don't ask how it could be accomplished, or begin to list all the reasons why it is impossible or impractical. Many advances have seemed impractical at their inception, and the visionaries have often been objects of derision

---

Imagination is the world.

Albert Einstein

---

and ridicule. The Wright brothers were seen as impractical dreamers, or worse. They had a vision that heavier-than-air flying machines were possible.

They had nothing to support that Vision. No one had ever successfully built one before; in fact, there had been hundreds of failures. An aviation pioneer named Langley had come close. Well before the Wright brothers, he had built a machine that was superior to theirs in many respects. Langley in fact was so close that modern aeronautical engineers believe that his machine would almost certainly have flown had he only made one or two more attempts. But he became discouraged after a crash and abandoned his research.

The Wright brothers were not aeronautical engineers; they were bicycle makers. They had no idea how to make a flying machine, but they allowed their thoughts to soar. They were not limited by visions of machines traveling around on the earth; they were able to envision machines in flight. They held this vision and then set out to build a flying machine, even though they had no practical evidence that it was possible. They simply knew inside that it *was* possible.

The Vision came first; the practical steps followed. Without the Vision, the practical steps would not have been taken. Who would undertake the risk and expense of building an airplane if they did not believe it was possible to fly? The Vision itself creates the practical steps necessary to manifest the reality. We are the creators, the manifestors of our dreams. To be is to create. We have been designed to develop our world, to manifest something out of nothing. We will create regardless of whether or not we are aware that we are creating. We can choose to become conscious of what we are manifesting in our lives, and create for our own good and the good of others.

The Wright brothers stuck to their Vision despite disappointments and setbacks. Eventually the physical reality conformed to their Vision, and they were credited with being the first men to fly. How different our lives would be today without them and people like them. Your Vision is worthy of the same depth of commitment, dedication, and belief in your dream. Don't stifle or doubt your Vision. Let your mind take wing; let it travel where it might and enjoy the trip. The more outrageous your destination, the better. If you accept in good faith the information your Vision gives you, you hold the power of the outcome. Through Vision the universe tells you what is possible in your

---

Winners expect to win in advance. Life is a self-fulfilling prophecy.

Anonymous

future, what greatness you can accomplish. You can then accept or reject those wonderful possibilities. You can always stay where you are–or take the risk and go where your soul leads.

A recent television movie told the story of Dr. Mary Groda Lewis. She is now an award-winning doctor, but she started out spending her teenage years in a juvenile detention center, characterized as a trouble-maker and an inadequate learner. Because of some very special, caring people in her life, it was discovered that she was dyslexic. With special help, and her own vision and determination, she not only overcame the roadblock of dyslexia, but the blocks of poor self-image, obstructive people, prejudice, and ignorance on the part of others.

She decided as a young adult that she would be a doctor in order to relieve some of the pain she had observed in the world. She held that Vision through long, hard years struggling against poverty, ill health, and the people who did not believe in her. Her Vision was so powerful that nothing on this earth could stop her from achieving her dream, not lack of money, lack of youth or lack of stamina–*because she acknowledged no lack in her life.* She succeeded even beyond her own expectations and became the outstanding graduate of her medical school. Dr. Lewis lives her Vision.

Vision Generates Personal Power

When we live our vision, we are invulnerable. As we use our imagination and keep our focus, we are empowered. When we live our Vision we do not allow worry into our reality. We take responsibility to dissipate worries as soon as we notice them. Worries and fears keep us off target; they dissuade us from our dream and pull us from our Path. There is no place for worry in imagination and envisioning. When we become willing to release worry from our consciousness, we see the rightness of our Vision. Worries and fears lose their strength quickly when we align ourselves with our Vision. When we are focused we have strength in our minds and in our bodies. Aligned with our Vision, we are empowered.

The muscle testing exercise from Chapter Two showed that when we focus our energy inward, toward ourselves and our fears, we are measurably weaker than when we focus outward, toward our dreams and joy. Forward focusing, or seeing the successful outcome of our goals, helps us get there.

What the mind can conceive and believe, it can achieve.

Napoleon Hill

For each of us, imagination is unique and personal. It is the pull toward desires and dreams, an unfoldment of our possibilities. We have demonstrated to ourselves the power of our own minds over our behavior. Now we will translate the power of our personal Vision into a set of goals or steps that we can take to accomplish our Vision.

Exercise
Vision in Action

- Allow about 15 minutes for this exercise.
- Find a comfortable place where you will not be disturbed.
- Relax in your chair and begin to clear your mind.
- Breathe slowly and deeply, allowing the relaxation to continue.
- Begin to imagine yourself living your Passion. Notice what you are doing and how you feel.
- Visualize the successful outcome of your travels toward your success.
- Once your successful outcome is clear in your mind, begin to walk slowly backward away from that moment and move back toward today. Keep your eyes focused on the future as you notice each step you have taken to get to your goal.
- As you walk backward, take note of all of the steps that led to accomplishing your outcome. These steps will serve as guideposts or milestones toward your success.
- Once you have returned to today, relax a moment and then start walking slowly back toward your successful outcome. Notice each step again along the way.
- When you arrive once more at your success, enjoy the thrill of the moment.
- Relax totally and when you feel comfortable, open your eyes.
- Record the steps that you took to reach your goal. This process gives you some basic guidelines or ideas for reaching your success and developing your action plan.
- Record the steps below or in your personal journal.

Steps toward my Vision:

_____

_____

_____

_____

_____

_____

_____

Repeat this exercise as many times as necessary to clearly visualize the steps you have taken. Each time you do it you will notice more clues and information than before. Everything you need is already in your brain; you simply need to gain access to it.

If you picture yourself as president of your own company, it will happen. If you picture yourself running a ranch for the physically challenged, it will happen. If you picture yourself as an artist, it will happen. However, if you picture yourself as a failure, or stuck in your life, that will also happen. Remember to guard your thoughts at all times, since it is your thoughts that create your life.

Using the energy of visualization for your greater good requires discipline and commitment. If you want to be a writer, picture yourself sitting at your writing table or your computer. See yourself enjoying the process of writing: the creativity, the intellectual and spiritual struggle to convey your ideas. Picture the outcome of your dream: your book being useful to people. Picture yourself on talk shows, lecture tours, in bookstores signing your books. Picture whatever part of writing is exciting to you. If you prefer to write for your own personal growth and have no desire to be published, picture that. If you are writing in order to affect the consciousness of the entire world, picture that.

I originally wrote this book in response to requests from participants in my Pathwalkers groups for more material. My greater Purpose is to help people be all that they can be. My Passion is teaching. My Vision is to have this book help people to be all that they can be, or at least be influential in that outcome.

Use the excitement of your vision to energize you toward your goal. If you hold your desires clearly in your mind at all times, you will

The future belongs to those who believe in the beauty of their dreams.

Eleanor Roosevelt

allow no space in your mind for worries, fears, anxieties and all of the debilitating mental habits that you may have formerly practiced.

Your Vision will guide you unerringly toward success. If you believe in yourself, then so will everyone else. If you believe you have the courage to act, you do. If you believe you have the ability, you do. If you believe you are successful, you are. If it is to be, it is up to you.

Pathwalkers: Carrie and Mark Greenwald

Carrie and Mark Greenwald are two special people whose innovative ecological endeavors have had a significant impact on New York City's environment. They have done pioneering work in urban gardening, turning rooftops into oxygen- and fruit-producing natural environments that stand in stark contrast to the urban congestion around them. Their work with growing plants has paralleled and reflected their inner growth, and the growth of their relationship with each other. Carrie is a gardener and songwriter, and Mark is an architect, although they have found their tasks stretched far beyond the boundaries of these disciplines as they have followed their Passion. First Carrie, then Mark, talks about some of the life changes they have gone through in pursuit of different Paths.

Carrie: Eden Calls

"I am a gardener," says Carrie Greenwald. "I create Edens and spend the better part of my time in them. I realize now that this is what I wanted to do in my life even when I was working at my other heart's desire, writing songs and comedy. When the adrenaline-pumping pressure of songwriting got me on edge, I would retreat into seed catalogs! After a while, I headed for more and more sophisticated gardening books. In my fantasy life I sought that most precious and scarce commodity in New York City: a little plot of earth to plant. There were the parks, of course, and I often imagined finding a perfect spot where I'd start digging a garden and by the time the Parks Department found out, it would be so beautiful they'd let me keep it. But you can't really go around digging up public parks...or can you?

"One day I ran into a friend who was pulling a shopping cart full of garden tools and Miracle Gro down the street. 'They're giving away land on Broadway!' she joked. 'Go grab some!' And there it was: heaven–in the guise of a rubble-strewn vacant lot surrounded by chain-link fence.

"A stalwart group of neighborhood people had planted bulbs inside the fence, and the bright tulips and daffodils were a welcome contrast to the ruins they surrounded. The next step was a truckload of topsoil so that a few plots could be scratched out for marigolds and bachelor buttons. All you needed to get a plot was the will to give it a try. The garden key in my pocket unlocked a passion for gardening that burns as brightly today as it did all that first summer, when nothing could stop me and I couldn't stop myself."

The Lake

"The Tibetans have a saying: 'Where there's a lake, the swans will come.' The small group who started the garden were off to their jobs each day but they had already created the 'lake' and I plunged in head first. During the work day, when I should have been at my typewriter, I was planting and building walls and pathways and clearing more space for more gardens. In my mind's eye I saw the whole lot covered with gardens.

"As I was there day after day, I became the on-the-spot contact person for signing up new gardeners. The swans started showing up at the lake by the dozens. Eventually I stopped feeling guilty about being there and gave in to the feeling that I was exactly where I was supposed to be.

"That summer the lot became the Broadway Garden, a magnificent spectacle of 75 gardens, trucked-in compost and manure, a greenhouse, a thatched sitting area, railroad-tie bleachers and a stage for moonlight performances. We called ourselves the Garden People and we were true to our name. Gardeners and their families became an extended family. Ten years later the friendships still abide.

"In this garden my ten-year-old daughter Vanessa sat on a little bench made for her by a gardener and watched a tiny sage grow into a large and woody shrub surrounded by the bright flowers she'd planted from seed.

"It was here too that I met my husband Mark, a city planner who waved and smiled each morning on his way to work. We didn't know then that this garden would be the springboard for the work and life we'd share together.

"Like Mark, hundreds of people passed the garden every day. Rushing for the subway became less important than stopping for a moment to take in the arresting sight of this acre of color and fragrance and all that it evoked. Strangers smiled and talked to each other in the shared commonality that comes from sharing something of beauty.

"When the commuters were gone the 'street people' emerged, some dazed by drink or dope. As they looked through the fence at the garden, the door on emotions long denied and deeply buried often swung open. The power of the garden was surprising: on this lake we were all equally swans.

"One grimy woman grabbed my shirt through the fence and sang to me, assuming that if I was in a garden I must be kind enough to listen. A Vietnam veteran sank to the pavement in front of the flowers and through chattering teeth told stories of combat. Some wept as they recalled their mothers' gardens, or laughed at their own crazy visions.

"A young man did a Rain Dance during a severe drought and as he danced, clear skies clouded over and sheets of rain poured down while gardeners laughed and cheered. I still don't know if it rained anywhere else but that acre on Broadway. A woman from Ceylon built a *stupa* (a little shrine) of flat round rocks, piled one on the other. Someone else buried a crystal empowered at Giza; a neighborhood priest poured holy water from the river Jordan into the four corners of the lot. I met a Tibetan priest who taught me that my spiritual practice was faith and that the way I worshiped was through gardening. I would never again think that gardens were unimportant, that I shouldn't be doing this, or that it didn't make a difference. Gardens make it easy both to feel spiritual and to show it."

Transitions

"Then the news came that the garden was to be bulldozed to make way for a high-rise luxury condominium complex," Carrie recalls. "Though this seemed like the death of our efforts, something inside me knew that it was time to accept this and move on. My job was to be alert and to recognize the next step when it came along.

"As soon as I saw a grassy promenade in Riverside Park I knew this was 'it'–flat ground atop a hill, in full sun, sheltered by trees and with a view of the Hudson River. I saw the garden there. To me, it was already a living entity of lilies and iris and herbs and flowering vines— no matter that at the moment the walls were covered with graffiti, the benches were torn apart and the lamp posts smashed. No matter that it was a *public park*.

"The Parks Department broke with precedent, and gave us a permit to dig up the grass and put in flowers. They offered us storage for tools, and a water hookup for hoses. All our needs were being met because the garden was already there before we started. I began wondering which was the illusion–my vision or the grass I was standing on.

"We began to create the new garden. Lovingly, gardeners and neighborhood people dug thousands of plants and put them into carts and cars or hand-carried them the nine blocks to the new site.

"So many people were drawn to the new garden that it became a safe place for people to sit, walk and jog. The Parks Department targeted that area for restoration. The walls were cleaned, the original lamp posts replaced and the new benches were turned to face the garden. Eight years later the Garden People are still going strong and the English Country Gardens in Riverside Park have won numerous awards. They are more beautiful than ever. They are even more beautiful than I had imagined.

"With the gardens in the park under way, I began negotiations with the developer of the luxury condominium that was going up on the Broadway Garden site. I wanted to put in a rooftop community garden. The Garden People were happy with their new site and were uninterested in taking part in this one. I felt alone–but there was that vision again. I saw ponds and fish and fruit trees and lush gardens, although I was told that a roof-top that received light only from the north would be shady, windblown and inhospitable to plants, trees and humans.

"I called all the open space, greening and gardening advocacy groups in New York City. Since the developer entered the negotiations with an open mind and the intention of giving something back to the community, we had a focus. Steven Schwartz from the Trust for Public Land took the lead. Through his good sense and skillful negotiations, a 7,000 square foot rooftop, one flight up over a parking garage, became a Land Trust, structurally designed as garden space and generously endowed. It was all falling into place.

"Upon the heels of these plans, I got a call from Mark, my friend and neighbor. Mark had become associated with the Cathedral of St. John the Divine and he asked if I would come and 'do a garden.' The Very Reverend James Parks Morton, Dean of the Cathedral, was offering help and encouragement for a food-growing project and had allotted land on the cathedral close for this purpose.

"What happened next was more than a garden. Mark and I fell into step as a team. We began sharing the vision: a model organic-intensive vegetable and herb garden to supply food to the soup kitchen and men's shelter. We organized volunteer personnel to de-sod, double-dig and plant the site. They then designed and built a solar greenhouse and solar fish tank. We started the Neighborhood Kid Corps, lectured to Nutrition Education groups from Columbia University, worked with families from a nearby Settlement House and taught classes in the garden. Herbs and edible flowers, climbing roses and grapes, enormous vegetables of all sorts from Vietnam, Puerto Rico, China and even sacred Aztec grain flourished. Other things flourished too. One was a deep friendship with our mentor and pastoral guide Dean Morton. And along the way, Mark and I fell in love.

"Construction on the rooftop garden had begun: soil was hoisted to the roof and spread two-and-a-half feet deep. We put the word out that we needed help and again the swans came to the lake. This spring the Lotus Garden, named for the lily and fish ponds, celebrated its fifth anniversary. A New York newspaper wrote about the garden in a food column as the fruit trees were laden with peaches and cherries, the grapes ripened on the railings overhanging the street, and red currants, gooseberries, raspberries and blueberries were harvested from the Berry Patch. The Herb Garden buzzes with bees and an occasional hummingbird. The garden is full of color. It faces north but the open sky vault, reflective walls and crazy quilt sun patterns accommodate both sun- and shade-loving flowers."

The Magic Show

"Mark and I were married last year at the Cathedral," Carrie says, " in a garden of 10,000 bulbs we'd designed as a memorial to a friend and gardener. Vanessa, now 19, sat in the front row and my heart filled with love as I looked at her pretty smiling face and remembered her in the Broadway Garden.

"Mark and I went 'professional' when our first big design job turned out to be the Loeb Boathouse Gardens in Central Park. What was once an asphalt service yard is now a long and curving border of beautiful weeping cherries, dogwoods, flowering shrubs and thousands of flowers in staggered bloom from April to November.

"We now live in Creamery Cottage on a farm in Greenwich, Connecticut. We had imagined all of the things we wanted in the perfect place to live. We imagined the money to pay for it. As always, what we got was beyond our dreams. We imagine Vanessa doing her own imagining and we watch her taking steps toward her own heart's desires.

"We imagine the work we would like and fair payment for our work. We design rock gardens, woodlands, bog gardens, wildflower meadows, grand English borders, little courtyards and all else that our minds can conjure up. We accept work without fear. We see what could be possible and the pieces always fall into place. We don't worry about jobs that don't come through, as we trust that they are simply not for us and that something else is already there. And that is the very essence of our faith: *it's already there*. We take the steps as the path appears before us. We expect it and try to be ready for it. At times when we come home from work after a twelve-hour day, exhausted and caked with mud, we agree that what we do feels like a lot of work. But we are happy. We are happy, tired, muddy magicians secure in the knowledge that the magic is there in us all to create the Magic Show of our choice."

Mark: Adventures in Space

"Since childhood I have possessed an innate ability to think visually and to imagine in terms of interlocking, multi-dimensional structures," says Mark Greenwald. "I grew up reading a lot of science fiction. School and sports were fun, but I couldn't wait to leap into some alien or unknown world, most often in the future, where myriad possibilities lurked around every corner. Eventually my favorite books became those in which the author took the time to map out the ground rules of each new world...what it looked like, how it got there and, if the writer was astute, how the society knitted together. This carried more value for me than the plot did. I began to develop in my youthful mind a capacity for imagining whole systems. By distancing myself from my own surroundings and studying other whole civilizations, I found it easier to reflect back more clearly upon our own tiny planet, and began a lifelong romance with structural thinking.

"Meanwhile, I was a Jewish kid growing up in a mostly Catholic working-class town, and Sunday mornings the local ball field was always empty. I was not from a very religious family and the churches in town mystified me. I figured something pretty important must be going on in them to keep my friends away from the playing fields.

"This curiosity created an interest in religions that only began to make sense to me while I was at Cornell University. I took a break from my architectural studies in order to investigate medieval Jewish and Arabic philosophy. That byway led to a totally unexpected insight into the history of science and culture. It wove together a whole new map of civilization right here on this planet that was as electrifying as any alien world I'd ever read about. In Plato and Aristotle, the men who had conceived the very underpinnings of Western science and art, science and the religions of the East and West intertwined. God lurked in mathematics; sacred geometry in architecture. The whole world became mystical.

"I had already started to develop my own values, wondering what fiendish forces could possibly have led us into a vacant culture of split-level ranch houses and shopping centers. An idea thrust itself upon me. After so many years of wondering, a startling realization occurred to me: Yes...I have a religion! I suddenly felt like a preacher beckoning his flock out of the desert of environmental demoralization that had claimed our cities and suburbs.

"Yet my religion was filtering through my intellect only. Something was missing. While my intellectual development was moving toward a peak, I quit one architectural firm after another. My sense of purpose took on the aspect of tilting at windmills; my emotional self was at low ebb and my spiritual side had not yet appeared. I had my doubts whether it ever would. I had gone through all of the sixties and half the seventies without one genuine mystical experience. I would suffer a great disappointment if my whole life was to be mystically barren.

"I flipped between the mainstream and the periphery during those days; from architect to graphic artist, radio announcer to community activist–my options got a workout. Being close, but never really falling off the edge, turned out to be a good confidence builder in the long run, but in the midst of it I was going half crazy under the glut of information I was taking in. I was constantly looking for the thread that would tie it all together for me."

Understanding and Mapping the World

"The structural thinking that I developed as a kid had done some evolving," Mark explains. "My architectural education had taught me how to look for patterns in three or more dimensions, how to visualize mathematics in terms of natural and pleasing proportions, but I just couldn't seem to find a meaningful application for such skills. In my mid-twenties in New York City, adrift in a sea of knowledge, I was lacking any real Passion or Vision in my life.

"Then, miraculously, I came upon a whole school of kindred thinkers: the French Structuralists: Barthes, Foucault, Ariés–intellectuals whose writings on the cultural antecedents of our everyday institutions really tickled my imagination, nudged my mapmaking and structuring abilities beyond bricks and mortar and into more subtle dimensions. Clear images of how things fit together–people, institutions, value systems and fields of knowledge–started drifting in.

"I was particularly inspired by the historian Fernand Braudel, who had illustrated, in his seminal work on the sixteenth century Mediterranean, how our natural and manmade worlds intertwined through many levels of history. Being in New York, I quickly likened this important new perspective to our subways, envisioning a world comprising *local time* and *express time*. We live our day-to-day existence in local time, stopping at each station to catch every little detail (i.e., the news).

"Express time co-exists with local time. If we can find a way to step back from the rush of daily events, viewing the world at a different speed, we can then glimpse some of the larger structures, like institutions and value systems, that tie those 'events' together. This is the perspective of express time. A further step brings us to the threshold of *natural events*. The trick to switching lines on this railway, I surmised, was to find the transfer stations. While mine was merely a possibility in my head at the time, I knew that others had found theirs through meditation, devotional practices, or work disciplines.

"This transcendental view of the world, combined with my prior intellectualized view of the mystical world, and the information gathered through my sojourns in and out of express time, all began to have meaning in my spirit as well as my intellect. I was slowly getting grounded. This generated faith in my own life's journey. It enabled me to subsume many of the fears that occur in ordinary life and to neutralize those things that might be perceived as personal failures or omissions. With this weight of stress removed, finding and recognizing my Passion and Vision became much more likely.

"Shortly before my twenty-eighth birthday, I picked up Dane Rudyar's *Astrology of Personality*. Mr. Rudyar and I speak the same language of maps and diagrams, my favorite way of 'seeing.' Within hours I had begun to view and assess the structure of my own life and answer a lot of questions about my elusive spiritual self. Rudyar's astrological structures made sense to me and much of it fit into my knowledge of sacred geometry. Moreover, I took heart in learning that I was entering my second full birth cycle of twenty-eight years and that if I'd missed the spiritual boat the first time, I had a fresh shot at it now. What timing! For the first time I was beginning to see how all the heady constructs my imagination had brought forth related to the complex world within me. I realized that my true passion was mapmaking!

"Within the year I finished my education as a city planner and went to work for the New York Department of City Planning. I saw and made yet more maps of how things worked, in and out of government, and I stayed in that job for five years. I learned how to subtly push and pull on policy strings until changes were under way. I learned that it sometimes takes a hundred tiny explosions to effect one major shift, and that you do not always see the direct results of your efforts. I acquired some tools relevant to my own Purpose. Then my intuition told me it was time to move on."

Fields of Dreams

"Back in local time, in my own neighborhood on Manhattan's West Side, I had become involved in reclaiming and starting a community garden on a large rubble-strewn lot. This was where I met Carrie, my wife and partner, who anchored this new garden on a daily basis, and who was to be my partner in a hundred other ventures. Like the mysterious churches of my childhood, I intuitively knew this lot was important to me as I passed it every day on my way downtown. Its changing patterns of usage became the theme of my Planning Law thesis.

"I had observed how the garden, was bringing new brightness to neighborhood lives. I realized that the ability to grow things is an important cultural infrastructure, something American city planners have overlooked in their zeal to build housing, commercial and transportation systems.

"When Dean Morton of the Cathedral of St. John the Divine offered me the cathedral's backing to establish a research garden and solar greenhouse aimed at reclaiming city rooftops and other spaces for growing food and flowers, I jumped at the chance. Here was an opportunity to effect planned change from the bottom up, through example, as opposed to the top-down kind of planning I had been doing for the city. 'Let the periphery take the lead from the center,' I thought, 'and perhaps this time gardens will push policy.' Carrie and I spent the next several years building and running this garden. We set up the new rooftop Lotus Garden where the Broadway Garden once stood and we mapped out other programs.

"As our vision and faith more closely coincided, Carrie and I grew closer as well. I experienced the long-awaited convergence of my three poles of existence–intellectual, spiritual and emotional. Working with our hands in the soil had a more civilizing influence than any other city planning or architecture job I'd ever done. There is something about the dignity attached to growing things for yourself and others that outstrips all other urban experience. It comes straight from the heart and that is what makes this work so appealing and so important. My vision was built upon sensing my place in the shifting structures of the world. Gardens are a centering or balancing mechanism in us all. They also happen to be a good transfer station between local and express time. They are inherently meditative and at peace with the world around them.

"Carrie and I continue to design gardens for business and pleasure. In local time we operate with landscape architects, contractors, arborists, nurserymen and other tradespeople. In express time we operate almost exclusively in the realm of people's dreams and society's aspirations. That covers a very wide field. My delight as a mapmaker is to forge people's dreams into the earth, while helping to move gardens toward an equitable place in the larger visions of society and structures of our everyday world."

The Action Plan

Living our Passion requires that we demonstrate in action what we came here to do. This part is easy, because our Purpose and our Passion are what we want to do and love to do most. Sometimes, though, after a lifetime of living off-purpose, it is a little hard to get on track, and the action plan is designed to get our feet firmly planted on our Path. By now you have identified your Purpose and your Passion. You have seen the vision of what your life looks like when you are acting on your Purpose. At this point you are all set to identify the first step to take toward your Path.

Our Pathwalkers Ken Blanchard, Larry Wilson, Barbara Peace, Charles Garfield, Thea Alexander, Lucy Beale, Carrie and Mark Greenwald, Joyce Filupeit and the others throughout the book, are all aware that plans must be made. If we do not give some form to our dreams they will remain in our heads and not be fulfilled. We must put energy into our desires. We must create action to fulfill our dreams.

Action plans guide our steps. They include starting points and route markers to indicate how we are progressing. They are not road maps of the only Paths available to us; they are suggestions, guidelines, alternatives.

Without an action plan we could be in danger of leaving our wonderful vision in the picture center of our heads. If we hold a picture

A journey of a thousand miles begins with a single step.

Old Chinese Saying

in our minds but do not commit to action, we are left with wishes and excuses rather than changes in our lives. Action plans are really physical representations of our contracts with ourselves to stay on target and in focus.

Mahatma Gandhi was a man with a plan. His mission and Purpose were so clear and directed that everyone could observe the powerful conviction behind his actions. He demonstrated consistency of values and purposeful integrity throughout his lifetime. His actions spoke eloquently of the fact that his Purpose never wavered. There was never a doubt that this was a person who knew what he was about and what he was here for.

Gandhi was here to fight injustice, and to fight it with non-violence and love. He said, "In my humble opinion, non-cooperation with evil is as much a duty as is cooperation with good." This statement was the bond that held his action plan together. Although he was abused, brutalized, and jailed repeatedly, no one could humiliate or destroy him because of the clarity of his intent and Purpose. He was at peace with himself always.

Whether our service is to our nation, to our patients, to our family or to our customers, each of us needs to be clear in our direction. This requires a plan. Business people know that success comes from a commitment to the basics, stated in the form of a business plan. Sales training courses teach salespeople to create an action plan. Any good researcher, architect, entrepreneur or minister has an action plan. Without an action plan you will get somewhere—but maybe not where you wanted to go.

We have come to this Adventure Step to meet our responsibility to commit to action. Living our Passion requires that we demonstrate in action what we came here to do. Each of us truly wants to live our Purpose and our Passion; only fear has stopped us. Now we have conquered our fear. This stage is exciting and energizing because we now move to a higher level within ourselves. Following this step we will never be the same because we know that all is possible. We understand that we are in control of our lives.

It is vital to remember that your life *is* your Path. The process is as important as the goal. If you do not enjoy the way, the process toward the goal, then reaching the goal will not serve your soul. It is our total involvement in the challenges before us that makes life worth living, not just the ultimate goal.

The Journey Is the Joy

On my thirty-second birthday I was given the gift of an opportunity to jump out of an airplane. I had some friends who were sky divers and I had been watching them with interest for two days. They gave me fifteen minutes of instruction in parachute landing falls and unintentional water landings. I jumped off of a chair a few times, hit the ground and rolled–and I was a graduate!

We flew to 5,000 feet and I was told to move to the doorway and stick my feet out. This was the first surprise, for when you stick your feet out of a moving plane they suddenly are wrenched sideways from the knees. At that moment someone tapped me on the shoulder (the signal to jump). I yelled "Geronimo!" and I was out the door. I was lost in space for the first few minutes, amazed by the feeling of being so high above the earth, alone. A little later the noise of the plane was gone and I found myself floating through the air in total silence. I looked up to make certain my chute had opened properly and then settled down to enjoy the trip. It was so quiet, so peaceful, and I marveled at the experience. A small bird flew by and sang, I felt like singing too, but I preferred the silence.

There was no sensation of falling as I was not yet parallel to anything close to the ground. It was just me and space. As I drifted closer to the earth I could tell that I was falling faster than I had sensed. I did not want the trip to end; I could have stayed up there forever.

I looked down to find the landing site and realized that I was drifting toward the Colorado River. I started thinking about my five-minute lesson on unintentional water landings. The instructor had told me that most people died because they would not let go of their equipment. I tried to remember, if they said to release it at 500 feet, fifty feet, or five feet above the water. Five feet sounded the most reasonable. I wondered how I was going to pay to replace all of this equipment!

As the winds died down I realized that I would not make it to the river, I would be landing in a ravine. It looked scary but I thought I could do it. Then I saw a new wrinkle: three rows of power lines from Hoover Dam. These were the same power lines that had been claiming the lives of local eagles. They looked huge, and I wondered if there was any way to keep from falling into them.

My mind processed all of the possibilities: (a) getting past the lines, (b) releasing my chute and falling through the lines, and (c), holding on to one line until rescued. Not one of the possibilities seemed feasible.

Feel the fear and do it anyway.

Susan Jeffers

After I had anticipated all possible options I suddenly realized that there was no way out. I was going to fall into the power lines and I was going to die. My first thought was, "Damn, I've almost finished my Ph.D." The second thought was "With electrocution, it should be fast."

As I fully accepted that I was going to die I was suddenly enveloped in a sense of total peace. I looked down at the earth and saw perfection and beauty. I realized that there was a greater Purpose to life than I had ever imagined. I understood that there was in fact a Grand Design and that we were all a part of it. I understood about good and evil. At that moment I felt my whole self floating within a great light, a white light that was less a cloud than simply an atmosphere. I knew that I had taken life much too seriously, that I had always been goal-driven and had missed subtle paths along the way. I knew that none of it had mattered except my time with people and the sheer joy of living. I knew that we were truly all one. I was totally at peace.

At about fifty feet above the earth, ground winds caught my chute and lifted me so that I just barely cleared the power lines. I skimmed across the lines and landed right next to them in a ravine.

I was gloriously alive.

I lost most of that deep sense of knowing very soon after being fetched back to the group. But one idea stayed with me: "Enjoy the process." Be here now. Live your life every moment you have because you never know what might happen next.

I made a contract with myself that I would never go to bed on any day without having done something wonderful, something enjoyable. I called it my "in case I get hit by a truck" contract. I decided that if I got hit by a truck, I didn't want to be thinking as the wheels rolled over me, "Oh, no, I never did this, that, or the other." The journey is the joy and every day is the journey. The action plan is guided by the awareness that our greatness lies in being fully present for every moment of our lives, and not in some grand final goal.

Each of us has our own Path, our own way to go in life. Each of us will discover the magic of our Path as we travel it. Action plans give us guideposts to check as we move along. In preparation for your action plan it is appropriate to reaffirm your commitment to your Purpose and your Passion.

Affirmation
Reaffirming Purpose and Passion

- Go to a quiet place. Quiet your mind by breathing slowly, deeply and comfortably.

- Clear your mind by picturing the healing and cleansing colors in your mind from blue to green to yellow to white.
- Remember the power of your Purpose and Passion that you discovered earlier. Allow this to flood your whole awareness.
- Write a concise statement of your discoveries below:

My greater Purpose in life is:

_____

_____

_____

_____

What I love to do most, my Passion, is:

_____

_____

_____

_____

With total clarity of mind and from the fullness of my heart, I embrace my Purpose and my Passion.

You are ready now to build your action plan with the magical elements of your own internal awareness, your positive self-talk, your ability to envision and your courage.

Formulating Your Action Plan

Step one is to state your dream. Write down your desired outcome.

> *To unfold one's truth within oneself is the lifelong aspiration of every human soul.*
>
> Tagore

For example:
> I want to be a successful artist.
> I want to help achieve world peace.
> I want to own my own business.
> I want to be a minister.
> I want to humanize the banking industry.

Record your dream here:

_____

_____

_____

_____

When you saw your Vision in the last chapter, you saw your goal and then walked slowly backward from the outcome to today. You observed the steps and made note of the actions you took to reach your success. Use these notes now to create your action plan.

Examples:
> First I went to art school.
> First I wrote to world leaders and asked them to support world peace.
> First I worked in the business I wanted to run and learned more about it.
> First I interviewed ministers and found out more about the commitment the job would require.
> First I learned banking.

Your first logical step:

_____

_____

_____

_____

In addition to knowing what our first step should be, we need to formulate alternative first steps to provide options to keep us going.

Many times we get bogged down because our first step doesn't work out as planned. Having alternatives helps to keep us on track.

Three alternative ways to take the first logical step:

1. _____

_____

_____

2. _____

_____

_____

3. _____

_____

_____

Sometimes our pathways are easy and sometimes we face apparent roadblocks. These roadblocks are really challenges or opportunities for creativity. We can also prepare in advance for some of these opportunities.

Examples of challenges:
I am told by the art schools that I apply to that I have no talent.
I meet with rejection when I talk about world peace with people.
I find out that the majority of people who start small businesses fail.
I discover that many ministers are leaving the field because of a crisis of belief.
I discover that I don't want to start at the bottom in banking.

We pray by moving our feet.

Mennonite saying

Challenges I may face are...

_____

_____

_____

_____

Take this opportunity to identify the particular resources, including your Master Mind group, that will help you to overcome your challenges.

Examples:

I recognize that many great artists were at one time told that they had no talent. I believe that I do have talent. I will get opinions and information from more sources.

I do not have to accept rejection; it is up to me. I will contact more people and do more networking.

Most small businesses fail because people give up too soon. I will read about or interview people who have succeeded. I will find help when I need it from other professionals, from the Small Business Association, and from contacts in the industry.

I need to test my own faith, not someone else's. The question is: do *I* want to be a minister. I will apply to ministerial schools.

I may not want to go through the banking industry per se; I may want to become an expert in financial consulting and affect the industry in that way.

Resources to help me overcome these challenges:

_____

_____

Winners focus on past successes and forget
past failures.

Denis Waitley

_____

_____

_____

Additional resources that will help me:

_____

_____

_____

It is important to set a completion date for your first step in order to give parameters to your commitment.

I will complete this first step by (date) _____

There are many rewards for accomplishment and one of them is the way that we feel when we have completed something. Record how you believe you will feel when you complete step one.

Examples:
I never thought I could do it.
I feel empowered.
I feel in control of my life.
I feel like a tiger.
I feel marvelous.
I feel relieved.

When I achieve this goal I will feel:

_____

_____

_____

Don't wait for your ship to come in; swim out to it.

Anonymous

222 Adventure Step Seven

This process concludes the first step toward your goal, When you have completed the first step you will be able to use this process for each subsequent step toward your goal.

In order to make your life work for you, you must commit to it. All of your energies and beliefs must be dedicated to the fulfillment of your greatest desires. Be very clear on what you really want. Identify the strengths that will aid your cause. Identify and challenge any barriers to your success. It is this process that determines what your life is really all about. Your life is your personal journey and no one else's. No one else can live your life for you or determine your Purpose and your Passion. Once you have given yourself this gift, you possess something more valuable than all the wealth in the world: the gift of yourself.

Affirmation
Putting It All Together

Before you leave this book write one final affirmation statement that ties all of your other affirmations together for you.

Examples:
I live the power of my life at each moment.
I am secure in my faith in myself; I know that I can accomplish all that I want.
I love life and I am filled with the joy of it.

Your Summary Affirmation:

_____

_____

_____

Plan for the future, because that is where you're going to spend the rest of your life.

Mark Twain

Congratulations! You have had some great adventures and worked hard in the course of reading this book. Hopefully you have also had fun, and experienced the high level of energy that comes from personal awareness and self-knowledge. You are now in control of your life, your work and your personal fulfillment. You have found the great, creative YOU!

Pathwalker: Joyce Filupeit

If you were ever to meet Joyce Filupeit you would not be surprised to learn that she is in control of her life, but you would be very surprised to find out that she ever felt that she wasn't. Joyce is outgoing, assertive, well-directed, intelligent and beautiful inside and out. She is a corporate consultant, wife, mother and race car driver.

Until I really got to know her, I would never have believed she harbored self-doubts. Joyce reminds us that we all have the dark side of our fears, and the business of life is to control that dark side so that our lives conform to our dreams rather than our nightmares.

Claiming Your Path

"The words quoted below from the Egyptian Book of the Dead are good descriptors of the path I've taken," says Joyce Filupeit. "If anyone had told me 15 years ago that I would be an independent consultant, training and working with large companies, I would have laughed myself silly. At that time I was in a dead-end job, stuck in a joyless marriage and internally I felt totally inadequate. Today I feel alive, tranquil, filled with enthusiasm and I am married to a man who loves and values me.

"Somewhere along the path I finally decided that I needed to take charge of my own life. I found that the 'White Knight' didn't exist, I was my own white knight. So I took a job at a large company even though I had no experience in that area. I had to really push myself through the fear and found that with my energy and intelligence I could 'fake it till I made it.' And the job opened doors for me, I was now visible in a large company. I discovered my long-buried interpersonal negotiating and coping skills.

"When a position opened up in the human resources department, I took it. Even though it was a lateral move in terms of money, it gave me the chance to use and develop more skills.

"I still hadn't really focused on where I wanted to go but I sure knew where I *didn't* want to be. I was learning.

I am not afraid of tomorrow, for I have seen yesterday and I know today.

The Egyptian Book of the Dead

"It soon became clear to me that working with adults in a training environment was 'home.' In a few years I was promoted to manager of human resources and I began an intensive set of training classes for the supervisors in my department. I loved all the pieces of this work: design, gathering material and especially the classroom.

"I started going to seminars that expanded my skills and I started reading everything about training and management theory I thought would be helpful. I realized that although I liked the other pieces of my job, training was my calling. So I volunteered for more and more classes to sharpen my skills. I also decided I wanted to train and consult full time.

"An opportunity came up sooner than I had thought possible, an opening in the training department. Even though it was again a lateral move, the experience and exposure were exactly what I wanted and needed. I set a target date to leave the 'paternal' environment of a big company. I felt I had to stay there until my youngest son graduated from high school–three years away."

Formulating the Action Plan

"I mapped out the skills and experience I felt I still needed, and the ways to get them. I kept reading everything I could and accepting any and all opportunities to speak and train," Joyce explains.

"Gradually I built up my self-confidence and my reputation internally within the company. I wanted to try 'outside' groups, so I joined a community service group and did sessions for them. I taught for the local community colleges, and I loved it all!

"I was becoming increasingly discontented with the necessary restraints and confines of a big company. I had several very good friends who were consultants and kept assuring me I could do it. I kept edging closer to leaving.

"It always amazes me that when things are supposed to happen, they just work out. All at once, just before my son graduated (my target date), we found a wonderful house in a beautiful area and I got a job offer from a consulting company in town.

"It was really extraordinary: all of my work was coming together. All the reading and seminars, all of the introspection to address my fears and concerns. All of it jelled at once. I had gradually baked a

---

A person first starts to live when he can live outside himself.

Albert Einstein

beautiful cake, adding essential ingredients, carefully, gradually, and suddenly-there it was!

"I'm still 'baking' but the future is lovely, busy and tranquil all at once and filled with what *I* want to do. After all these years, how wonderful."

References

A Cosmic Book: On the Mechanics of Creation by Itzhak Bentov. Destiny Books, Rochester, Vermont, 1988

Anatomy of An Illness by Norman Cousins. Bantam, New York, 1981

Changing the Game: The New Way to Sell, Larry Wilson, John Wiley and Sons, 1988

Don't Tell Me It's Impossible Until After I've Already Done It, Pam Lontos, Willam Morrow and Co., Inc., NY, 1986

How Shall I Live? by Richard Moss, M.D. Celestial Arts, Berkeley, 1985

Intuition Workout by Nancy Rosanoff. Aslan, Boulder Creek, California, 1988

Man's Search for Meaning by Viktor E. Frankl. Washington Square Press, New York, 1984

Peak Performers: The New Heroes of American Business by Charles Garfield. Avon, New York, 1986

The Power of Ethical Management by Ken Blanchard and Norman Vincent Peale. William Morrow, 1988

The Road Less Traveled by M. Scott Peck, M.D. Touchstone Books, New York, 1978

The Win/Win Way by Lucy Beale and Rick Fields, Harcourt-Brace Jovanovich, 1987

Superlearning by Ostrander and Schroeder. Delta, New York, 1977

2150 A.D. by Thea Alexander, Macro Books, 1976

Vibrational Medicine: New Choices for Healing Ourselves by Richard Gerber, M.D. Bear and Co., Santa Fe, 1988

Waking Up: Overcoming the Obstacles to Human Potential by Charles Tart. Shambala, Boston, 1987

Work With Passion by Nancy Anderson. Carroll and Graf, New York, 1984

Communing with the Spirit of Your Unborn Child
by Dawson Church

"Wow! This book is incredible! An amazing book, a beautiful theme, well written and produced!"
—*Ken Carey, The Starseed Transmissions*

This "excellent" book, "an outstanding addition to prenatal literature" (Midwifery Today), is a clear how-to manual for parents exploring pregnancy, birth and infancy from a spiritual perspective.

Using photographs, diagrams and meditations, this powerful, inspirational classic outlines in simple, practical language a step-by-step approach that enables parents to communicate with the inner magic of the unborn child.

Available as a book or audio tape.
Also sold as a set for a $3 discount.

$8.95 book, $9.95 tape

Intuition Workout   by Nancy Rosanoff

This practical training manual teaches simple techniques to access our deepest sources of inner knowing in any situation.

The author, one of America's outstanding corporate trainers, shows that intuition, like a muscle, is strengthened by training. She outlines dozens of case histories and step-by-step exercises proven effective even with "non-intuitive" people.

"A workout in cultivating our inner resources and building self-confidence. Once you know how to do it, you can adapt the techniques to any situation."
—*New York Daily News*

Available as a book or audio tape.
Also sold as a set for a $3 discount.

$9.95 book or tape

Meditation for Children by Deborah Rozman

This is a new updated edition of the bestselling classic on growing a close, nurturing family. These simple methods teach children to relate to life with new confidence and joy.

"...successfully integrated yoga, concentration, meditation, creative fantasy, movement, psychology and —most assuredly—love in a way that clearly shows interested adults a path to fulfilling children's spiritual needs...many positive side effects occur...a heightening sense of community, a sense of trust between adult and child, an ability to focus energy, greater creativity and a calm confidence."
—*New Age Journal*

$9.95

The Heart of the Healer
Edited by Dawson Church & Dr. Alan Sherr

A collection of outstanding figures on the leading edge of conventional and holistic medicine, including Bernie Siegel, Norman Cousins and Prince Charles, draw on their deepest personal experiences to explore how we get in touch with the essence of wellness. This classic has been called "Exceptional" —*SSC Booknews*; "Thought-provoking" —*Publisher's Weekly*; "Profound...provocative" —*Ram Dass*.

$14.95

Voice Power
by Dr. Joan Kenley

The sound of your voice can have more than five times the impact of the words you say. *Voice Power* shows you how to draw on the resources of your whole body to release your natural voice—the voice that is truly and fully you. It shows you how to integrate the deepest roots of your personality, your vitality and your sexuality, to project charisma and confidence.

"...a fun read as well as a very practical, thorough book." —*Network Magazine*

$18.95 Hardback

Love is a Secret
by Andrew Vidich

What is God's love and how do we experience it? Drawing on the words of saints and scholars from a rich variety of religious traditions, from Taoism to Christianity, from Sufism to Judaism, this book illuminates the psychology of humankind's deepest spiritual experiences.

"In a world yearning to find its unity and connectedness, this book invokes for all to hear, 'Love has only a beginning, my friend; it has no ending.' "
—*Dr Arthur Stein, Professor Peace Studies, Univ. of R.I.*

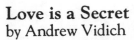

$9.95

The Unmanifest Self
by Ligia Dantes

This book, like a warm, gentle friend, guides us toward an experience of self-transformation that is quite different from our usual waking consciousness, that is vastly more than an improved version of the old self. *The Unmanifest Self* teaches us the art of *objective self-observation*, a powerful tool to separate the essential truth of who we are from the labyrinth of thoughts and emotions in which we are often caught.

"...beautiful and inspiring." —*Willis Harmon*

$9.95

Order Form

(Please print legibly)   Date _____

Name _____

Address _____

City _____ State _____ Zip _____

Phone _____

Please send a catalog to my friend:

Name _____

Address _____

City _____ State _____ Zip _____

Quantity Discounts!

$2 off 2nd item
$3 off 3rd item
$4 off 4th item, etc...

Item	Qty.	Price	Amount
Communing With the Spirit of Your Unborn Child (book)		$8.95	
Communing With the Spirit of Your Unborn Child (tape)		$9.95	
Intuition Workout (book)		$9.95	
Intuition Workout (tape)		$9.95	
Meditation for Children		$9.95	
The Heart of the Healer		$14.95	
Voice Power (hardback book)		$18.95	
Love is a Secret		$9.95	
The Unmanifest Self		$9.95	

Subtotal	
Quantity Discount	
Calif. res. add 6.5% sales tax	
Shipping	
Grand Total	

Add for shipping:
Bookrate: $2.00 for the first item, $1.00 for ea. add. item
First Class/UPS: $4.00 for first item, $2.00 ea. add. item
Foreign: Double shipping rates

Check type of payment:

☐ Check or money order enclosed

☐ VISA   ☐ MasterCard

Acct. # _____

Exp. Date _____

Signature _____

Send order to:

**Aslan Publishing
310 Blue Ridge Drive
Boulder Creek, CA 95006**

or call to order:

**(408) 338-7504
(800) 372-3100 US or
(800) 423-5784 In California**

Order Form

(Please print legibly)   Date _____

Name _____

Address _____

City _____ State _____ Zip _____

Phone _____

Please send a catalog to my friend:

Name _____

Address _____

City _____ State _____ Zip _____

Quantity Discounts!

$2 off 2nd item
$3 off 3rd item
$4 off 4th item, etc...

Item	Qty.	Price	Amount
Communing With the Spirit of Your Unborn Child (book)		$8.95	
Communing With the Spirit of Your Unborn Child (tape)		$9.95	
Intuition Workout (book)		$9.95	
Intuition Workout (tape)		$9.95	
Meditation for Children		$9.95	
The Heart of the Healer		$14.95	
Voice Power (hardback book)		$18.95	
Love is a Secret		$9.95	
The Unmanifest Self		$9.95	
		Subtotal	
		Quantity Discount	
		Calif. res. add 6.5% sales tax	
		Shipping	
		Grand Total	

Add for shipping:
Bookrate: $2.00 for the first item, $1.00 for ea. add. item
First Class/UPS: $4.00 for first item, $2.00 ea. add. item
Foreign: Double shipping rates

Check type of payment:

☐ Check or money order enclosed

☐ VISA   ☐ MasterCard

Acct. # _____

Exp. Date _____

Signature _____

Send order to:

Aslan Publishing
310 Blue Ridge Drive
Boulder Creek, CA 95006

or call to order:
(408) 338-7504
(800) 372-3100 US or
(800) 423-5784 in California